Public Justice,
Private Mercy

Public Justice, Private Mercy

A GOVERNOR'S EDUCATION ON DEATH ROW

Edmund G. (Pat) Brown

WITH

Dick Adler

WEIDENFELD & NICOLSON

New York

Published by Weidenfeld & Nicolson, New York
A Division of Wheatland Corporation
841 Broadway
New York, New York 10003-4793

Published in Canada by General Publishing Company, Ltd.

Excerpts from *Death and the Supreme Court,* copyright © 1961
by Barrett Prettyman, Jr., reprinted by permission of
Harcourt Brace Jovanovich, Inc.

Library of Congress Cataloging-in-Publication Data

Brown, Edmund G. (Pat), 1905
Public justice, private mercy.

1. Capital punishment—California.   2. Death row—
California .   I. Adler, Dick, 1937–   .   II. Title.
HV8699.U5B76   1989   365.6'6'09794   88-36278
ISBN 1-55584-253-4

Manufactured in the United States of America

This book is printed on acid-free paper

Designed by Irving Perkins Associates

First Edition

1   3   5   7   9   10   8   6   4   2

Contents

Acknowledgments

The authors would like to thank the following people for their help in bringing this long-awaited project to final fruition:

Van Gordon Sauter, who acted as godfather and midwife; Marcia Legere Binns, who did much of the early groundwork; Bernice Brown, Jerry Brown, and Kathleen Brown Sauter, who shared their memories; Jane Wilson Adler, who read and advised on early drafts; Senior Editor William Strachan of Weidenfeld & Nicolson, who counseled wisely; Ann Sausedo of the *Los Angeles Herald Examiner* and Joseph Somora of the California State Archives, who dug deep into their files; Judges Cecil Poole, Arthur Alarcon and John S. McInerny, former clemency secretaries who generously helped recapture the past; Janet M. Carter, Drena Ribeiro, Michael Benedict and others at Ball, Hunt, Hart, Brown and Baerwitz, who gave time and encouragement; and Michael G. Millman of the California Appellate Project, who opened the gates of San Quentin for us.

Prologue

On a cool, sunny morning in February 1988, I finally repaid an old debt and visited Death Row at San Quentin Prison for the first time. The debt was to the thirty-six people I let go to their deaths during the eight years I was governor of California. Now I wanted to talk to some condemned prisoners and find out if anything had changed.

There hadn't been any executions in California for twenty-one years, but they were expected to begin again very soon. So many prisoners were under sentence of death and so much pressure had been building around them over the last few years that I fully expected to see dark clouds of anger and fear hanging over San Quentin. Instead, I found a prison population that had somehow managed to make the probability of death as much a part of its routine as the weekly movies.

I had been to San Quentin many times before, in one official capacity or another, but I'd never visited Death Row or witnessed an execution. Back in 1945, during my first term as district attorney in San Francisco, I was invited to attend the execution of a prisoner who had been successfully prosecuted by my office. I told a couple of homicide detectives involved in the case that I planned to attend, and both of them quickly urged me not to. When I asked them why not, these tough veteran police officers told me that if I did, I would never be able to push for a death sentence again.

I took their advice and didn't go, then or later. And during the next several years of my public career, I managed to give the death penalty my full support. As district attorney, I pressed for it routinely in virtually every capital case. As California's attorney general for another eight years, I made it my business to see that the death penalty as the judgment of the court was carried out. In fact, I supported it so strongly that on one occasion I even came close to going to jail for it. While I was attorney general, a judge gave Caryl Chessman a sixty-day stay of execution, one of the many stays that this champion jailhouse lawyer received during his eleven-year legal fight to stay alive, and I made some ill-chosen comments to the press about softheaded judges who let convicted criminals push them around. My remarks were widely quoted in the newspapers, and the judge quite rightly saw me as being in contempt of court. He was ready to jail me for it, too, until I called him and apologized profusely.

I had some moments of doubt about the death penalty during those years, of course. The man I beat in my first election for district attorney had never tried a capital-punishment case in his twenty-four years in office, and I made a big point of that in my campaign. When I was running for reelection, my staff pointed out to me that I hadn't yet tried a capital case myself, and that this fact might be used against me. I told them to get me a lead-pipe cinch, and they found a case of two young men who had gone in with loaded guns to rob a service station on Market Street. When the owner fought back, they shot and killed him.

They were defended by an old lawyer who hung around the Hall of Justice hoping to pick up work, and he did a good job for them. In his closing argument, I remember him saying, "I know the evidence against them is overwhelming. But my clients are only twenty-one and twenty-two years old, with no previous records. We haven't seen Mr. Brown here in court for some time.

You know why Mr. Big Cannon himself is here today? Because if you give my clients the death penalty, Pat Brown will be re-elected."

He was right, and when I got up to make my closing argument, I admitted it. "I do have some qualms now about asking for the death penalty," I told the jury. "So what I want you to do is walk out of here, elect a foreman, and come back in thirty minutes with a verdict of guilty and a recommendation of life in prison without possibility of parole. Let those two young men know they've killed somebody and that they're going to spend the rest of their lives behind bars." The jury did just that, and I never tried another capital case.

What happened to a man named Burton Abbott also made me think seriously about the death penalty while I was attorney general. Abbott, a twenty-seven-year-old accounting student at Berkeley, was convicted of the kidnapping and murder of a fourteen-year-old girl in 1956. Abbott lost all his appeals, was turned down for clemency by Governor Goodwin Knight, and was set to die in the San Quentin gas chamber on March 15, 1957. Until this point, I looked at Abbott as just one of the several capital cases that I, as the state's chief prosecutor, was moving through the mills of justice.

On the morning of March 15, Governor Knight was on his way to the naval air base at Alameda for a cruise around San Francisco Bay on the aircraft carrier *Hancock*. Just an hour before the original 10 A.M. execution time, Abbott's new attorney, the flamboyant but very able George T. Davis, succeeded in reaching Governor Knight at the Navy base by making a statement on a live television program that he knew Knight might hear. The governor called Davis, who asked for a stay of execution so that he could present a new appeal on a constitutional point to Chief Justice Phil Gibson of the California Supreme Court. Knight agreed to delay the execution for an hour.

It was 10:40 A.M. when Gibson read and turned down the appeal. By the time Davis finally reached Governor Knight by radiotelephone on board the *Hancock*, it was already after the

11 A.M. deadline. Davis asked for another stay, to make another appeal to a federal judge. Knight finally agreed; he called his clemency secretary, Joseph Babich, in Sacramento and told him to inform the prison.

Babich's call to Warden Harley Teets was logged in at 11:20 A.M. He asked if the execution had begun, and was told that it had: two minutes before, at 11:18, Warden Teets had given the signal to drop the cyanide pellets into the sulphuric acid. The deadly gas had already begun to rise when Babich's call came through. It was too late to stop Abbott's execution. A prison official later explained that even if they sent in men with gas masks, they risked endangering the lives of spectators outside.

During the public uproar that followed Abbott's death, I called a press conference and asked for a five-year moratorium on the death penalty in California. My thinking was that incidents like this proved just how vulnerable to human error the current system was: we needed time to examine and reform the system. Like other requests for a moratorium before and since, it was a failure.

My moments of doubt, however, seemed to fade into the background when I became governor. Taking office in 1959, I was almost certain that I knew how I felt about the death penalty. To me it was a necessary evil, a deterrent against certain kinds of violent crime, especially those committed with a loaded gun, and a needed emotional purge for society. Most of all, the death penalty was the law of the state, one of the laws I had sworn to uphold. If I disagreed with a law, it was my job to try to change it through the legislative process, not by evading my responsibility and refusing to enforce it.

Looking back on it now, I'm sure that I *was* worried about my own reservations concerning the death penalty when I became governor. That's why I went out of my way to pick three hard-nosed, pro–capital-punishment former prosecutors as my clemency secretaries. That's also why I insisted on conducting every clemency hearing myself, often sending out investigators to collect more information if I thought some area still needed clearing up. But at the time, these worries were effectively pushed aside by the bustle and politics of everyday life in office.

In my eight years as governor, I was obliged to consider fifty-nine death-penalty cases. I was the last stop on the road to the gas chamber for these fifty-nine people. After much deliberation, I sent thirty-six of them to death and granted clemency by commuting the sentences of twenty-three others to life imprisonment without possibility of parole, far more than any previous governor of California. Earl Warren, who had been governor for eleven years, made just six commutations and let eighty-two prisoners die. Knight, my immediate predecessor, also granted clemency in just six of the forty-seven cases that came before him.

A few of those twenty-three people whose death sentences I commuted went on to leave prison because of changes or loopholes in the law and lead normal, successful, productive lives. One man whose life I spared eventually got out of prison and killed a woman. Even now, twenty-five years later, I still can't decide whether I would have let those twenty-three prisoners die if it meant saving the life of that one woman.

During my two terms as governor, because of my high percentage of commutations, I became known as an outspoken foe of capital punishment. It wasn't an image I consciously tried to create; in fact, the evidence is strong that it seriously damaged my political future. Richard Nixon made it such a major issue during the 1962 gubernatorial campaign that at one point I was sure I'd lose and seriously considered dropping out. In 1966, the death-penalty issue did help Ronald Reagan defeat me for governor, thus launching one political career and effectively terminating another.

When I left office, there were sixty prisoners on San Quentin's Death Row. There were no executions during my last three years, because the U.S. Supreme Court had ordered retrials in the penalty phases of most capital cases still under appeal, but new death-penalty prisoners continued to be processed and sent to the Row. During Governor Reagan's two terms, only one man was executed: Aaron Mitchell, convicted of killing a policeman, was gassed in 1967. And in 1972, when the U.S. Supreme Court ruled that the death penalty as practiced in California and certain other states was "cruel and unusual punishment" and therefore unconstitutional, Death Row as such ceased to exist. Famous condemned prisoners like Charles Manson and Sirhan Sirhan had their sentences commuted and were transferred to other parts of the prison, or to other prisons.

Then, in 1976, the Supreme Court reversed itself: individual states *could* decide to impose the death penalty for crimes involving special circumstances. California acted quickly. State Senator George Deukmejian, long an advocate of capital punishment, led the fight to get a new law on the books in 1977. My son, Governor Jerry Brown, vetoed it, but the legislature overrode his veto. And in 1978, when a proposition to toughen and expand Deukmejian's law won an overwhelming 71 percent victory at the polls, Death Row was formally back in business.

By February 1988, there were 224 men awaiting death at San Quentin. The years of delay and indecision appeared to be over. Rose Bird, Jerry's choice as chief justice of the California Supreme Court who had voted to reverse all fifty-seven death sentences that came before her, had been removed from office along with two other justices who were thought by the public to be against capital punishment. Executions had already resumed in Louisiana, Texas and Florida: virtually everyone inside and outside the prison expected California to be next. The gas chamber was tested and declared off limits to tourists. Some public defenders, in what writer Michael Kroll labeled the "cancer ward effect," had even quit their jobs rather than take on death-penalty cases as ordered. They said that the virtual certainty of having to watch one of their clients die was more responsibility than they were prepared to handle.

These feelings were very much in the air as I talked with several Death Row prisoners on that February morning. One of them, the third man on the Row after it reopened, had been there since 1978. He had watched it grow from the original sixty-four cells—now called the North Segment, or North Seg—to include a South Segment and part of another whole section. He told me that the original six condemned cells were now known as quiet cells—not punishment or isolation but a place where a prisoner can have more privacy. This simpleminded, friendly man seemed proud to be in one of those cells, and was also proud to be part of the group of prisoners who in 1980 won a consent decree that regulated the way in which men on Death Row were treated. Before the consent decree, I was told, condemned prisoners were locked down in their cells virtually twenty-four hours a day. They were stripped, searched and handcuffed on the way to the showers every other day. Since the decree, they've been allowed to exercise and mingle with other condemned prisoners.

I asked one man, who seemed intelligent and articulate, if all the public debates and changing laws about the death penalty played a large part in the condemned prisoners' lives—if indeed temperatures on Death Row were reaching the boiling point, as some media stories indicated. "We don't talk about it much," he told me. "The main topics of conversation here are pinochle, movies, food, what goes on in the Yard. The Rose Bird election didn't make much of a stir inside; there certainly hasn't been the rising tide of anger or frustration that I've read about in the newspapers. I think those stories get spread by some prison officials who want us to screw up. Lots of people would love to break up North Seg, get our privileges taken away. It's easier to kill people you hate."

The men on Death Row used to be able to work, like other prisoners, but the program was shut down in 1987 because of the growing number of condemned. The men I spoke with wished it would begin again; they missed the activity as much as the small amount of money they earned. The work was a good way to use up anger, one man said. Now he lifted weights to get rid of his. Some men painted pictures. Others joined gangs, made secret knives, got into fights.

I asked the prisoners if they had developed any other survival techniques during their years on Death Row. One man put it most succinctly: "I always try to remember that the guy I'm talking to has killed somebody."

All the men I met on Death Row had one thing in common: they had been found guilty of capital crimes and faced official execution. Otherwise, they were as diverse a group as you might find in any prison community. Most of them insisted, with varying degrees of intensity and believability, that they were innocent. One case in particular seemed to have enough doubt and possible unfair application of the law surrounding it to warrant serious investigation. Several of the prisoners, even if guilty, had been in prison so long and had led such quiet, peaceful lives that the idea of executing them now seemed incongruous. Even the one man who loudly proclaimed his guilt and his desire to die looked very much like someone who should be protected from himself.

As we were leaving, I looked around North Seg one last time. Although the numbers had been changed, some of the cells still held great historic meaning for me. Over there was the one that used to be Cell 2455, made famous by the title of the first book by Caryl Chessman, the man who almost ended my career as governor. Down the way was 2440, the cell where Machine Gun Walker tried to strangle himself just before his first date with the gas chamber. Richard Lindsey, whose case still troubles me the most of any I have had to deal with, spent his last months just over there. Farther along were the cells where John Crooker, Edward Simon Wein, Leo Lookado, William Cotter, Clyde Bates and Manuel Chavez waited for me to act.

The clemency decisions were only a small part of all the things that happened during my eight years as governor of California: there were major changes in the shape and fabric of society, the effects of which I still witness every day. But as the years passed and I entered my ninth decade, those fifty-nine life and death choices began to loom larger and larger, until by the time of my visit to San Quentin my head was full of questions about them. What had I, as a governor and a man, really learned from those decisions—about the death penalty itself and the way we punish the worst members of our society? Could I, by going back to the records and trying to recall the passion and the discord of those days, come up with some contemporary truths to help other public officials who now and in the future will have to make similar choices? And, finally, the inevitable, ultimate selfish question: have my decisions on Death Row really made any difference?

This book is an attempt to answer those questions.

Public Justice, Private Mercy

CHAPTER ONE

The Law Student

You tend to collect a lot of unusual things over a career of more than fifty years as a lawyer and a politician. Statues, hats, stuffed animals and objects made or carved from every known substance cover all the available spaces in my office and home, and thousands of other things burst from boxes in closets and libraries.

One of the strangest items in my collection looks very prosaic indeed: a 107-page typed and roughly bound manuscript of a play called *M'Naghten's Madness*. It's not a particularly good play, and as far as I know it has never been staged anywhere. Producers and audiences would probably find it too dogmatic and predictable in the way it lays out the facts surrounding the nineteenth-century case of Daniel M'Naghten, the Scotsman who killed a British parliamentary secretary and whose subsequent trial redefined the idea of criminal insanity. But what makes *M'Naghten's Madness* so unusual is that it exists at all. It was written in 1963 by John Russell Crooker, Jr.—a man who was scheduled to die in San Quentin's gas chamber in 1959.

John Crooker became an important part of my life the day after I took my first oath of office as the thirty-second governor of

California. January 5, 1959, was a marvelous day, starting with my opening address to a joint session of the state assembly and senate. The Republicans had squabbled among themselves, nominating the conservative Senator William Knowland for governor and forcing the popular incumbent, Governor Goodwin Knight, to run for the U.S. Senate. So the 1958 election turned out to be a glorious landslide for our side, a result which I said in my speech "reaffirms our conviction that the people of California are resolved to move forward with courage and confidence. . . . Clearly, then, our duty is to bring to California the forward forces of responsible liberalism."

That night, the victorious Democrats celebrated with two inaugural balls. Congratulations and high hopes flowed as easily as the California champagne. The next morning, still charged with those emotions, I met with my new cabinet and talked about the goals of what was only the state's second Democratic administration in the twentieth century. My four grandparents had come to California in the 1850s; my father, an Irish Catholic, and my mother, a German Protestant, had both been born here; and I had already been in public office here since 1943. I felt confident that I could handle the responsibility of being governor, but also very fortunate that I'd been given the chance.

Late on the afternoon of that second day, January 6, my clemency secretary, Cecil Poole, who had been chief assistant district attorney in San Francisco, came into my office. He apologized for interrupting my plans for the future, but reminded me that on Friday, January 16, we had an execution scheduled. If I intended to hold a clemency hearing, he needed to know now, so that he could set a date and bring in the district attorney and the defense counsel.

I took a deep breath. "Look, Cecil, we both know that I reached the height of my popularity as governor *yesterday*, when I took the oath of office," I told him. "Now that I have to start making decisions which won't please everybody, there's nowhere to go but down. Couldn't we postpone this particular one for a few days, so I can at least get started on some of the legislation I want to push through?"

4

Poole repeated his regrets, but said that if I intended to move on this, he needed a quick decision. I asked if he'd had a chance to study the file. Not as thoroughly as he planned to in the future, Poole told me, but enough to know that the case had been all the way to the U.S. Supreme Court on appeal, where it was turned down. And there was a note from Governor Knight saying that he had carefully examined the case and couldn't find any grounds for executive clemency.

I asked Poole who the original trial judge had been; he told me it was Stanley Mosk. I knew Mosk well: he had just succeeded me as attorney general. I also knew that he was not only an excellent jurist but one of the most compassionate men I had ever met, a staunch foe of capital punishment, a judge who would go out of his way to find a reason for not giving a convicted felon a death penalty. If Mosk had reviewed the trial transcript and found the sentence just, there was little room for doubt. "That's good enough for me," I said. "I don't see any reason at this stage to stir things up. We'll let the execution proceed as planned."

That night, our second in the creaky old Victorian Governor's Mansion on H Street in Sacramento, my wife Bernice asked me about the things that I'd done on my first actual working day as governor. I told her about the meetings and plans that had filled the day, and as I was talking, I began to have some second thoughts on the way I had dealt with the upcoming execution.

I knew that Governor Knight had made his final decision on the Crooker case in 1957. Wasn't it part of my job as governor to at least read the file and see if any new information had come to light in the last two years?

The next day, I asked Poole for the file on Crooker. I hadn't decided yet about a clemency hearing, but it wouldn't hurt to spend a few minutes seeing what was in there.

Like almost everyone else in California who read the newspapers, I knew the basic facts of the Crooker case. It was hard to avoid the headlines during the summer of 1955: "Socialite Killed by Houseboy Lover!" shouted the tabloid headlines. Even the usually staid *Los Angeles Times* ran a giant banner which said,

"See Blackmail Motive in Divorcee's Murder." Some writers compared the case to a Raymond Chandler story; others found the setting straight out of James M. Cain or F. Scott Fitzgerald.

The file filled in the details. John Russell Crooker, Jr., was a handsome, studious, hardworking Navy veteran of twenty-nine when he came to Los Angeles from his native Maine in 1953 to study law at UCLA. The school's placement bureau sent him to a couple named Norma and Frank McCauley, who were looking for a live-in houseboy. In return for some light duties—tending bar, helping to look after the couple's three young children, doing odd jobs—Crooker got a room in the family's elegant home on Somera Road in the expensive Bel Air neighborhood above Sunset Boulevard, all his meals, and a small amount of cash. And, as the McCauleys' marriage began to break up and the husband moved out, Crooker also received—for a time—the affections of the petite, attractive thirty-one-year-old wife. Crooker eventually left his job as Norma McCauley's houseboy, and her feelings toward him changed first to boredom and then to outright fear. But he never gave up on the idea that they were still lovers.

On the morning of July 5, 1955, I read in the file, the family maid sent five-year-old Kirk McCauley to wake his mother for breakfast. "You'd better go in," the boy said when he returned. "Mommie is in a mess." In a bedroom that had been torn apart, Norma McCauley lay facedown on a blood-soaked chaise lounge, still wearing the red cocktail dress she had put on for a party the night before, her arms crossed under her head. She had been stabbed many times. A white stole decorated with rhinestones was wrapped tightly around her neck and knotted on one side.

For the first few hours, there appeared to be other possible suspects in Norma's murder: her estranged husband, several recent dates. But one character in the drama soon began to take on special interest for the police as they interviewed the dead woman's friends—the former houseboy who had been Norma McCauley's lover but who lately had been behaving very oddly. At one-thirty that afternoon, two Hollywood detectives went to 5128 Marathon Street, got a key from the manager, entered

6

Apartment 205 with guns drawn and arrested John Russell Crooker, Jr.

Crooker at first denied any knowledge of Norma's murder. He asked repeatedly to be allowed to call an attorney, refused to take a lie detector test, and in general flaunted his own small and recently acquired knowledge of criminal law to the increasing anger of the officers questioning him. Finally, after more than twelve hours of grilling, he caved in and said, "Well, I will write it out for you." In red ink on yellow paper, Crooker wrote his seven-hundred-word confession, telling how on the night of July 4 he had parked his own car at UCLA, taken a cab to the Somera Road house, entered the house and hid in a closet for several hours, smoking and even urinating in a glass until Norma came home from a date. "Norma was stunned to see me but she remained remarkably calm and self-contained," Crooker wrote. "I, on the other hand, was extremely nervous and generally unable to make myself realize that I was there in her room and had taken the means described to see her. . . ."

Crooker wrote that he and Norma had talked for over an hour, he trying to get her to tell him why she wouldn't see him, wouldn't answer his calls and letters, and she refusing to discuss it and gradually beginning to doze off. "I didn't know what to do," he wrote. "For days and days I had not known what to do. I had tried threats and coercion and profession of my feelings for her. She had rebuffed all my attempts and now she was going to sleep?"

On the dresser in Norma's bedroom, Crooker wrote, he found "a small kitchen about ten inches long with a blade about six inches." A police officer reading each page as Crooker finished it pointed out that the word "knife" had apparently been left out after the word "kitchen," so Crooker went back and inserted the word. "I put the knife in my coat pocket and knelt beside her for what seemed to be a long time. She was asleep. I took her throat in my hand and she awoke and started to scream." Hearing the maid stir in the next room, Crooker wrote, he put his hand over Norma's mouth, took the knife from his pocket and stabbed her

7

several times. "She still made sounds and struggled on the lounge. I choked her more with some clothes around her throat and after a long time she was still and the house was still, and I couldn't realize that Norma was gone. . . ."

Crooker concluded his confession with details about taking Norma's keys and some money from her purse, walking back to his car, driving home and burning his clothes in the incinerator. "Somewhere along the way I must have thrown out her keys and the knife because I didn't have them in the things I threw in the incinerator," he wrote. Before he was allowed to go to sleep, officers drove him out to the Bel Air house, walked him through the crime and collected physical evidence from the closet where he had been hiding.

The next morning, the file told me, Crooker was questioned by Los Angeles District Attorney Ernest Roll, who was worried most about the missing knife. Crooker talked openly until he got to the part about entering Norma's house. Then he refused to continue and asked again that he be allowed to call an attorney. Roll placed a call for him to Raymond Simpson, a Long Beach lawyer who had been Crooker's instructor in a legal history class and subsequently became a social acquaintance. "Do they have the right to use any physical force to have me continue with the questioning?" Crooker asked Simpson. They did not, Simpson told him. "I see," Crooker said. "Well, probably they will attempt to continue with the questioning, and probably to avoid the force I will have to talk with them." District Attorney Roll, who had been listening on an extension, told Simpson he had advised Crooker that he didn't have to answer any questions, and denied that any force was being used. Crooker told Simpson that he had given the police a statement in which he had "tried to express myself as well as possible. There are holes that I cannot fill and they insist that I fill them." Simpson arranged to meet Crooker at the jail at seven o'clock that evening. After that meeting with Simpson, Crooker repudiated his confession, insisting that it and his other statements to the police had been obtained against his will.

The events surrounding Crooker's confession and his repeated requests to be allowed to call a lawyer played a large part in his trial and subsequent appeals. Crooker's defense was that he had indeed gone to the McCauley house and had hidden in the closet to confront Norma—but on the night of July 3, not July 4. She had told him that someone else was threatening her, but refused to name him. His defense attorney argued that without the confession the state had no case against John Crooker: no knife or keys or bloodstained clothes had ever been found.

At the end of Crooker's trial, the jury deliberated for a little over an hour before sending out a note to ask Judge Mosk if they could consider his confession valid even if they agreed that Crooker had asked for and been refused the right to call a lawyer. Mosk brought the jury back into the courtroom and reread them his instructions on that point—that the refusal to allow Crooker to consult an attorney did not in and of itself make the confession involuntary, but that the refusal could be considered by the jury along with all the other facts in deciding whether or not the confession had been given voluntarily. The jury chewed this over for another few hours, then took a vote that turned out to be unanimous in favor of a guilty verdict. The next vote, as to degree of punishment, was also unanimous—murder in the first degree, without recommendation of mercy. John Crooker, they said, should be sentenced to death in the gas chamber.

I put the file down for a moment and closed my eyes. It was obvious to me from what I had read that Crooker was guilty of the murder of Norma McCauley. He had confessed it in detail. But he didn't seem to have planned the killing in advance, or brought a weapon with him; it looked like a true crime of passion, the kind of crime which in a country like France would receive a much more lenient sentence.

On the crucial question of whether the confession was given voluntarily or coerced without benefit of counsel, I felt some sympathy for both sides of the U.S. Supreme Court's five-to-four decision. Justice Tom Clark, who wrote the majority opinion, said that any suggestion of coercion in the police refusal to let Crooker call a lawyer was negated by the defendant's age, intelligence and education—especially his knowledge of criminal law. Justice William O. Douglas, author of the dissenting opinion, disagreed, saying that "no matter how well educated and how well trained in the law an accused may be, he is sorely in need of legal advice once he is arrested for an offense that may exact his life."

But both the U.S. and California supreme courts had already voted against Crooker on the issue of the confession. I needed something else to justify holding a new clemency hearing.

As I understood it, the section of the California constitution that granted the governor the power of clemency—defined in my dictionary as "a disposition to be merciful"—had little to do with guilt or innocence, or even with the finer points of the law. The first was for a jury and the original judge to decide; the second was the job of the appellate courts. What I as governor had to look for was some extraordinary reason why the defendant should not be executed.

I found some justification for at least holding a new clemency hearing on the Crooker case at the very end of his file: a report from a three-man psychiatric committee that had examined John Crooker recently. They found that since his arrival on Death Row, Crooker's mental condition had been deteriorating—aggravated by reported homosexual overtures from the Row's most notorious occupant, Caryl Chessman. The chief psychiatrist at San Quentin, Dr. David Schmidt, had diagnosed Crooker's delusions and hallucinations as schizophrenic reactions and conversion phenomena. Crooker, he said, was "exhibiting a passive-aggressive personality, with partial or acute hysteria."

I thought for a long moment about my priorities as governor, about the fair employment bill I wanted to get through, the water and education bills I had in the works. Was the Crooker case really worth putting those things on hold and perhaps in jeopardy? Then I called Cecil Poole and asked him how soon he could set up a clemency hearing for Crooker. He consulted his calendar and told me that Friday, January 9, looked like the earliest we could get everybody together.

10

That was a week before the scheduled execution. "Do it," I said.

My first clemency hearing as governor quickly took the shape that all fifty-eight that were to follow it would take. Gathered in my office on the morning of January 9 were the parties involved: Crooker's attorney, one of his sisters, a psychiatrist from the state mental hospital system, some members of the press, Cecil Poole and myself. The Los Angeles district attorney's office had been notified, but declined to send a representative. They sent a statement for the record, however, pointing out that Judge Mosk had ruled several times in the past that he believed the crime *was* premeditated and the verdict of first-degree murder was justified. Since the jury had voted against life imprisonment, they said, no other punishment was proper other than the death penalty.

I'd already studied the so-called "Black Book" on the case, the clemency report put together by Poole, including the results of the investigation into Crooker's background and family history made at my request by the Adult Authority, the state agency in charge of prisoners and parole. There wasn't anything startling there, no single moment or cause to point to and say, "*That's* why he killed Norma McCauley!" Instead, what I found on those pages was a common catalog of human weakness and failure that nevertheless helped me to better understand what had happened.

John Crooker grew up surrounded by women—the only son in a Maine family of seven children. His father was a cold, somewhat tyrannical man who had once wanted to be an engineer but settled instead for working as a carpenter, painter, builder and insurance salesman. The senior Crooker frequently beat his children and his wife, a loving but downtrodden woman who always took her husband's side. The young Crooker was a chronic bed wetter, and despite medical attention this enuresis continued throughout his life: he was rejected by the Navy because of it in 1942, and was only accepted in 1945 when he persuaded his mother to write a letter stating that the condition had ended, even though it hadn't. Norma McCauley sent him to a urologist for treatment in 1953, but this, too, was unsuccessful. Then in 1955, after his arrest, the condition vanished abruptly and never returned.

I also learned that before meeting Norma, Crooker had a history of strongly emotional, often overdependent relationships with women. He had been married twice, and when the first marriage was ending, he attempted suicide by taking an overdose of phenobarbital along with a large quantity of whiskey and then slashing his wrist with a razor. A Veterans Administration psychiatrist diagnosed him as manic-depressive at that time but released him without treatment. In 1956, on Death Row, he began to suffer the severe hallucinations and periods of manic-depression that I had already heard about from the psychiatric committee.

In the report, the prison psychiatrists speculated as to why Crooker had killed Norma McCauley. He grew up, they said, feeling unworthy and rejected—desperately seeking the approval of women and then behaving in ways that insured his eventual rejection by them. When he met Norma, she quickly became the center of his life, offering not only a place to live and an instant family, but also sex and love in the bargain. When she, too, rejected him because of his childish demands for attention, it was more than he could bear. He snapped from the strain of this final rejection and killed her.

I began the hearing by telling everyone that I firmly believed John Crooker to be guilty of the murder of Norma McCauley, and that I didn't want to hear any arguments as to his innocence or guilt—the courts had already decided that issue. What I wanted to hear now were reasons why he should or should not die.

His attorney spoke of Crooker's life and character before the crime: how he had never been in any kind of trouble, had been honorably discharged from the Navy, had worked his way through law school. He stressed the point that when Crooker came to Norma McCauley's house that night, he didn't bring a weapon of any kind, thus showing that the conditions of premed-

12

itation and malice aforethought necessary for first-degree murder were missing. He also pointed out that the U.S. Supreme Court had been split five to four on the validity of Crooker's confession, so that it was not a clearly defined issue.

Crooker's sister spoke movingly about his good character and sweet temperament as a child, and about his obvious mental anguish during the last months of his affair with Norma Mc-Cauley. The state psychiatrist told of evidence that Crooker had been through a serious nervous breakdown after he got to Death Row, but said that he seemed mentally stable now.

I listened carefully to all they had to say, but what really made up my mind was a note from Stanley Mosk in the report, stating that as the trial judge he would not object to a commutation of Crooker's sentence from death to life imprisonment. "This defendant's crime arose out of relationship with the deceased under a set of circumstances that would not likely happen again," Mosk wrote. "He is an intelligent young man of some cultural attainment, and if personality defects could be cured or contained, he could in the distant future become rehabilitated and become a constructive member of society."

The hearing lasted about an hour. I told everyone that I would announce my decision on Monday, although in truth I had already made up my mind. "Cecil, I'm going to commute," I said to Poole when we were alone. "It's true that a young woman, the mother of three young children, is dead. But nothing I do can bring her back. The death penalty is supposed to be a deterrent, but I don't see how killing this young man is going to stop anybody else from killing their lover or ex-lover in a fit of anger. If he went in with a weapon, I'd probably let him die. But the fact that he didn't, plus the psychiatrists' report and Mosk's statement, give me the reasons I need to commute. Do you agree?"

Poole thought for a moment. This dedicated prosecutor—a Harvard Law School graduate and the first black ever hired as a deputy district attorney in San Francisco—felt a special responsibility for the effect that any decision of mine would have on the administration of justice in California. "It won't make you very popular with the police department or the district attorney's office in L.A. County, but otherwise I think you'll be okay," he said. Then we sat down to write the formal commutation of sentence which I released on Monday.

"The record clearly shows and I personally believe that Crooker is guilty of murder in the first degree," the commutation document said. "But his crime was caused by passion and emotional factors, and was not one committed for gain or perpetrated by cruel and sadistic methods. His psychiatric reports reflect some mental illness which undoubtedly contributed to his emotional blow-up. I also feel that had he pleaded guilty, his life would probably have been spared, and in this connection I am impressed with the sentiments expressed by the trial judge, the Honorable Stanley Mosk. . . .

"I have also considered Crooker's age, education, intelligence and general circumstances; the fact that he had never previously been in trouble, had no prior arrests, never exhibited any criminal tendencies, and was honorably discharged from the U.S. Navy in 1946.

"I am mindful of the considerations of orderly law enforcement, of even-handed justice, and of the great respect that must be accorded to the decisions of our courts and juries. And although I conducted a personal hearing in this case, I do not intend thereby to establish a policy in this respect. Each future case will be processed and treated as an individual matter. But under the circumstances of this case, I have concluded that the interests of society and justice will be best served by granting to John Russell Crooker, Jr., San Quentin No. A-34965, a commutation of sentence from death to life imprisonment without possibility of parole.

"In witness whereof, I have hereunto set my hand and caused the Great Seal of the State of California to be affixed this 12th day of January, A.D., Nineteen Hundred and Fifty-nine."

So John Crooker's commutation became one of the very first official documents I signed as governor. I heard later that Crooker's lawyer had deliberately delayed in filing for a review by the California Supreme Court until after the election, gambling that I would be a softer touch for clemency than Governor Knight. When a reporter asked for my reaction to that, I said, "Smart lawyer! Knight had already turned them down once—I sure as hell couldn't do any worse!"

As it turned out, my first decision about clemency was the easiest one I ever had to make. John Crooker was young, attractive and intelligent; his crime, although terrible, was at least understandable. There were, as Poole had predicted, a few grumbles from police and prosecutors in the Los Angeles area, mostly in the form of letters hoping that I didn't plan to establish any dangerous precedents. But they quickly faded away, especially as the Chessman case began to occupy more and more of the world's attention. And in spite of my fears, none of the important legislation that I'd put into motion seemed to be in danger.

On February 21, 1959, Crooker wrote me a letter that helped to ease any lingering doubts I might have had about my decision:

My dear Governor Brown:
Routine transfer and other requirements of incarceration make this my first opportunity for personally expressing appreciation for your act of commutation of the sentence of death given to me. Actually, I feel this expression will continue the rest of my life, as I continue to feel an obligation to show justification of your act of clemency.
My experience as a condemned person and now as one released from that ordeal has been sobering and quite revealing for me. Perhaps you will deem it appropriate if I give you a few of my thoughts at this time.
In the past and recently more frequently, news media have reported you, Governor Brown, in opposition to capital punishment. It seems to me, everyone who honestly and objectively considers this subject must eventually reach this conclusion: the death penalty is absolutely negative in our society, because it accomplishes little or nothing and costs so very much. It is also something quite terrible and inhuman in society and is violence carried to its illogical extreme.
I personally believe that people condemned to death contain some real answers to society's questions as to why people commit

15

capital crimes. But for the most those answers are allowed to die with them. Some of these people have even much more to offer of benefit to society, which is also lost by their being put to death. It could well be our hope that society will more and more recognize and, more important, treat *all* crimes as evidence of illnesses in individual human beings and in society as well. This appears to me to be an approach which is affirmative, and there appears to be so much to be gained from it, at a far less long-range expense for society. Such an affirmative approach will perhaps even become imperative, with the constant annual increase in crimes. At least, I would say without question from my own experience as respects capital crimes, the abolition of death as punishment would offer important and worthwhile opportunities for study, as well as treatment and, in some cases, rehabilitation. If this is true in these cases in which the crimes and the punishment are both so extreme, it must also be true in varying degrees for lesser crimes and punishments. And this would offer great hope against the negative concept of there being an inevitable and ever-increasing incidence of crime in society.

For my part, I will want the rest of my lifetime to at least be some proof of an amount of truth in these thoughts. It will be my hope that I will not only continue to justify your act of commutation, sir, but also give by my example some proof of the value of even a human life which was condemned, and, of the benefits to be derived from doing away with death as a punishment. This is an obligation I feel and will willingly accept as much as possible. Perhaps this will be some real expression of my great appreciation of your act as Governor of this State which has made my continued life possible.

Crooker later described even more eloquently how it felt to be sentenced to death and then have that sentence commuted in a statement written to be included in a 1961 book called *Death and the Supreme Court* by a Washington lawyer named Barrett Prettyman, Jr. "On Death Row," he wrote, "you never escape the thought of death. It is there in your mind, day after day, while you eat, while you play, while you bathe, while you walk down among the living for a visit, while you glance or stare out a window at the open sky, when you hear the sparrows chirping and see them gather around a window and fly out into the air, and while you

16

watch one after another of your fellowcondemned, your fellow-man, escorted by your cell, down toward the gas chamber, to be put to death. You never escape the thought—until months and months later, when the relieving gas rises to destroy your thought, and all of you.

"You awaken from the shock of the death verdict, unless you are one of those too sick in the mind. You begin to resist death, study your legal case, listen, talk, read this thing—the law—which has ordered you to be put to death. Day after day you do this, constantly, hour after hour. You learn something about this thing—the law: that it is not a fine, straight line from crime to trial to punishment; that it is a broad, waving line, where similar or worse crimes of the same type do not lead to the same punishment; that it is also a line of several links, in which each link has the power over the preceding link—only if you, yourself, usually poor and ignorant and friendless, can reach that next link, to seek to exert this power, by appeal, which is the link to life.

"You are one who never even thought of crime, much less punishment, and still less capital punishment, until after your crime. Or you are one who knew of the gas chamber and sub-consciously sought its relieving gas. Or you are one who knew of the gas chamber and consciously sought this way of suicide. You are probably one of those three, because condemned men who knew of capital punishment and calculated the gas chamber as a risk of their crimes, before their crimes, are relatively very, very few.

"You relive your crime many times, or approach near to it in your thoughts and then back away from it in horror, appalled by it. You would turn backward. You would show your remorse—as condemned men sometimes do, one to another—the remorse you hide with your fear in your heart and mind you would show to the one with the power and the given promise to understand and not condemn you, to the one you cannot find, unless perhaps you are a person who finds him in God.

"Waiting to be put to death is like having a charge of electricity attached to your limbs—not a big charge, but a small irritant charge to the nerve endings—constantly there and needling at any moment of the days or nights, no matter what you are doing, even awaking you from your sleep.

"It is like being immersed in water and taking an eternity to drown.

"That is what it is like to wait to be put to death—not just to me—but, I believe, it is to a large extent an unexaggerated statement of what almost all condemned men feel, whether or not they can express their feelings in so many words.

"Except among those who are too sick in their minds.

"And even those who are too sick in their minds experience much of what it is like to wait to be put to death, except that they do not resist death; or they welcome death; or they run and hide from it in dreams that do not last long enough; or they blindly curse themselves or their judges or their juries or their victims or their families or their societies or their worlds; or they fly through the windows with the sparrows and are gone long before the gas takes away their breath.

"That is what it is like to wait to be put to death.

"The day I was taken from Condemned Row—when I walked unescorted down among the living, rode in a bus along the highway, saw the open sky, the green grass and flowers, the men and women and children, the homes and places of business along the way, and breathed a relatively free air again—can only be described with accuracy as somewhat of a resurrection for me—an opportunity to begin now to build a life of real under-standing of myself and other human beings, training myself, with the help of psychiatric and other professional staff mem-bers, to live a healthy way of life in this new life given to me."

Crooker's feelings about himself turned out to be not only extremely well expressed but also accurate. Away from Death Row, under the care of psychiatrists like San Quentin's Dr. Schmidt, his condition improved rapidly. Crooker worked hard at his writing—my manuscript copy of *M'Naghten's Madness* is a product of that—and also was put in charge of the prison's elec-troencephalograph, the brain-scanning instrument that was to play a vital part in several of my subsequent clemency decisions.

Good reports about his progress continued to come in, and as early as 1964 I began to think and talk of commuting his sentence further, to life with the possibility of parole. My staff thought this was a bit premature: in a memo to me dated July 9, 1964, my last clemency secretary, John S. McInerny, said, "One of your strongest arguments in the death penalty controversy has always been that society has been amply protected in those commutations granted by you because you have carefully provided in each case that the sentence is to be *without possibility of parole*. None of the men you have commuted since becoming Governor have as yet had the restriction against parole imposed by you lifted. I believe that it would have an undesirable affect on your plan to eventually abolish capital punishment if you were to issue this commutation at this time. . . ."

I saw the sense in McInerny's argument. But letters urging further clemency for Crooker continued to come in, including one from the British writer Brigid Brophy, with whom he had been corresponding, and so as one of my last acts before leaving office at the end of 1966, I did commute his sentence to straight life. His annual visits to the parole board finally paid off in 1972, when he was released from prison.

One day in March of 1978, John Crooker and his wife dropped in at my office in Beverly Hills for a short visit. I saw before me a pleasant, well-spoken and obviously intelligent man in his mid-fifties. Our visit lasted perhaps twenty minutes: both of us had other matters to attend to.

A few weeks later, a letter from Crooker arrived on my desk. "I doubt that my own expressions of gratitude during our meeting quite equaled how I imagined such a meeting years ago," Crooker wrote. And he ended his letter with some words about his family and working life. "I don't really know whether there is any social contribution I should be making beyond just being sure these areas remain intact," he wrote. "If there is, perhaps it will evolve in some opportunity unforeseen now; and, if not, maybe just quietly living out the remainder of my lifetime with work and family is the way it's supposed to be. . . ."

I think I made the right decision.

CHAPTER TWO

The Bandit

It's hard to say which Caryl Chessman caused me the most trouble—Chessman alive or Chessman dead.

When my son Jerry, who had just left the Jesuit order after studying for the priesthood for three and a half years, called and urged me to do something, I gave Chessman a sixty-day stay of execution and tried to get the state legislature to declare a moratorium on the death penalty. For that, I was called every foul name in the book; my family was booed in public; my political stock fell so low that there was talk of a recall.

Then, when I followed the law and the will of the people and allowed Chessman to be executed, the reaction was equally intense. Today, twenty-eight years later, I still get abusive mail about letting an innocent man die.

If the Crooker case marked the beginning of my course of study on the death penalty, the Chessman case was my first major public test on the subject. Perhaps I had been subconsciously trying to avoid that test when, as attorney general, I did everything I could to move Chessman's execution through the legal process. I probably sensed, or at least feared, that someday down the road I would be the one who had to make the final decision.

I was just starting my fifth year as district attorney in San Francisco on that January night in 1948 when a twenty-seven-year-old small-time career criminal named Caryl Chessman was arrested, after a car chase and shoot-out, as a suspect in the armed robbery of a men's clothing store in Los Angeles. I'm not sure exactly when I first heard his name, but during the next several years the facts and fantasies surrounding his case certainly became a permanent part of my emotional baggage.

Chessman had been in and out of prison since he was sixteen, convicted of stealing cars and holding up liquor stores and gas stations, but this time he found himself in major trouble. The Los Angeles police had been investigating a series of "red-light" robberies and sexual assaults on the mountain roads above the city. A man roughly matching Chessman's general description had been driving up to couples in parked cars, flashing a red spotlight to make them think it was a police vehicle, then robbing the couples and forcing some of the women to perform sexual acts.

Chessman's stolen Ford car plus a penlight and .45 automatic found in it were similar to items used in the "red-light" crimes, and several of the victims identified him in a lineup. The police were sure they had their man; the story of his arrest made even the San Francisco papers. Despite his loud protestations that he had never been a sex criminal, Chessman was charged with several counts of robbery, two counts of sexual perversion and—most importantly—three counts of violation of Section 209 of the California Penal Code, the so-called "Little Lindbergh Law": kidnapping with intent to commit robbery. If bodily harm could be proved, Section 209 was punishable by a sentence of death.

Chessman was smart and cocky, and when a couple of lawyers he tried to hire told him that his defense strategy was weak and that he ought to consider copping a plea, he decided against the strong advice of the court to defend himself. Chessman insisted from the start that the police were trying to frame him because

21

he had been robbing bookies and brothels from which they were receiving protection money. He also said that he knew who the real "Red Light Bandit" was, but always refused to name him. All he had to do, he said, was prove his own innocence: catching the other guy was the police's business.

No matter what side of the Chessman fence you finally wound up on, it would be hard to argue with the fact that his trial in May 1948 was seriously flawed. Up against a forceful veteran prosecutor named J. Miller Leavy who quickly made it clear that he was going for the death penalty, and in front of a judge, Charles W. Fricke, who in the course of his career sentenced more people to death than any other judge in California history, Chessman needed all the legal help he could get. Instead, he stubbornly continued to defend himself, only reluctantly agreeing at the last minute to let a relatively inexperienced public defender sit at the counsel table and serve as his legal adviser though not as his counsel of record.

Heavily guarded as he arrived and left the courtroom and not permitted by Judge Fricke to move around it as Leavy did, Chessman had to stand behind his table and ask his questions. In this manner, he examined all the witnesses, many of whom had already identified him in lineups and who during the course of the trial made it obvious to the jury that they thought he was guilty. Limited in his access to law books and lacking any formal legal education, Chessman made many obvious mistakes and let several key motions slide by with little resistance. On the first day of the trial, he asked Judge Fricke that he be given a daily transcript of the proceedings. Fricke denied the request, although he had never before denied a daily transcript in a capital case. Fricke gave no reason for not doing so then, but in later years he claimed it was because prosecutor Leavy had not joined in the request. As many lawyers and writers have since pointed out, Leavy didn't need to formally ask for a transcript. A close friend of the court reporter, Leavy was accustomed to dropping by and asking him to type up the pages of testimony he needed— and his requests were always granted.

Chessman built his defense around alibi witnesses for the times of several of the crimes he was charged with, and various discrepancies—in height, coloring, visible scars, straight or crooked teeth—between himself and the descriptions of the "Red Light Bandit" given to the police by victims and witnesses. But Leavy was able to convince the jurors that the alibi witnesses were either confused or lying, and that the discrepancies were commonplace in criminal investigations. The jury came back after two days of deliberation and found Chessman guilty on all but one of the eighteen counts. On the three counts of kidnapping with intent to commit robbery, they found the crucial "bodily harm" present in two instances and recommended the death penalty for both.

Almost immediately after the verdict, the court reporter, an elderly man who had been ill during the trial, died before he could transcribe all his notes. Several competent court reporters reviewed the dead man's notebooks and concluded that, because of his illness and the outdated form of shorthand he used, they were virtually illegible. Although a California statute said that if a reporter died before transcribing his notes in a civil case a new trial must be held, at the time of sentencing Judge Fricke refused Chessman's motion for such a new trial. This was a criminal and not a civil case, the judge pointed out; the letter of the law must be observed. He sentenced Chessman to death twice for the kidnapping convictions, then added sixty-one years for the other counts.

Chessman arrived at San Quentin on July 3, 1948; he was led to Death Row and locked into Cell 2455, which would be his home for more than eleven years. From it, he mounted a massive legal and literary attack on the courts and on public opinion, designed to obtain a new trial and save himself from the gas chamber.

The chief weapon in Chessman's legal battle, the one which really kept him alive all those years, was the transcript of his trial. Four months after the first court reporter's death, J. Miller Leavy told Judge Fricke that he had found a man who could transcribe the garbled notes. The fact that this new reporter asked for and received $10,000 for the job—about three times the normal fee—that he happened to be Leavy's uncle by marriage and also had some serious drinking problems apparently didn't bother Fricke, but it gave Chessman and his legal advisers enough ammunition over the ensuing years to fire off petition after petition to Sacramento and Washington, D.C.

The newspapers kept me in loose touch with the Chessman case while I was district attorney. In 1950, I ran for the post of attorney general, linking myself with the incumbent Governor Earl Warren and avoiding an endorsement of the Democratic candidate, James Roosevelt. I was the only Democrat to be elected in the ensuing Republican landslide. In January 1951, I was sworn in as California's chief legal officer, and Chessman immediately became a part of my daily life. As the state's top lawyer, it was my job to come up with arguments against all of his petitions in state courts, which were frequent. In December 1951, the California Supreme Court turned down by a vote of five to two Chessman's appeal for a new trial. The court agreed that some of his arguments about the improper conduct of the judge and the prosecutor were valid, but ruled that this improper conduct was really Chessman's fault because he, in the words of the majority opinion, "deliberately and not naively determined to represent himself." Judge Fricke then set March 28, 1952, as the date on which Chessman should be put to death.

Beginning a pattern that was soon to become irritatingly familiar to law-enforcement figures across the state and country, Judge Jesse Carter of the California Supreme Court—one of the two judges who had voted in Chessman's favor on the appeal— gave Chessman his first sixty-day stay of execution while he petitioned the federal courts for a review. The petition was denied, a second execution date of June 27 was set, but just three days before that day a federal judge granted Chessman another stay while his whole case was reviewed. During this period, Chessman began work on his first book, *Cell 2455, Death Row,* a self-serving but dramatic and surprisingly well-written account of his life. The book was sold to Prentice-Hall, which planned to publish it on May 3, 1954, and with some of his first advance money Chessman hired a private detective and a pair of experienced criminal lawyers. His petitions and appeals slowly worked their way through the federal court system and were routinely turned down. In December 1953, the U.S. Supreme Court denied Chessman's petition for a review; in February 1954 the same body denied his request for a rehearing. Judge Fricke then set a third execution date: May 14, 1954.

Thinking back to my feelings about Chessman at that time, I'm sure they were mostly ones of anger and frustration. First of all, I was certain that he was guilty: a belief that I must admit hasn't changed to this day. Because of some shrewd maneuvers on his part and some admittedly dumb ones on the part of the judge and the prosecutor, Chessman had managed to obscure the fact of his guilt and make it an unimportant issue. I read his book, admired his writing skill and didn't believe a word of it. As to the question of whether he should die for crimes that didn't involve taking a life, I frankly didn't see that as any of my business. The courts had reached a verdict and a sentence; it was my job to have that sentence confirmed and executed. But every time my office tried to move the case to its conclusion, some judge or court seemed to throw another roadblock in our way.

In 1951, the California legislature had amended Section 209 of the Penal Code, making kidnapping harder to prove and granting parole eligibility to anyone who had previously been convicted under this section and sentenced to life without possibility of parole. In April 1954, a month before his latest execution date, Chessman used this as the basis for a clemency appeal to Governor Goodwin Knight, who had taken office the year before, when Earl Warren was appointed to the U.S. Supreme Court. Knight had already granted three reprieves from death sentences, the last two on the grounds that the men had not been convicted of murder. "I have a repugnance to take a life where no life had been taken," he said at the time. But in Chessman's case, he managed to overcome that repugnance and twice turned down Chessman's requests for clemency.

It was May 13, 1954, and Chessman had less than a day to live when one of his lawyers finally found a judge willing to listen to yet another plea for a stay on the basis of the flawed trial transcript. Judge Thomas F. Keating of the Marin County Superior Court, which had jurisdiction over San Quentin, granted a sixty-day stay, and that's when I went public with my angry comments, including one that this latest stay was "a perversion of justice." Judge Keating blasted back, even threatening to jail me for contempt of court, and I had to call him and apologize for my rash remarks.

Chessman had been brought very close to death three times, only to be snatched back at the last moment. This fact plus all the attention being given to his book stirred up waves of public emotion that soon moved the case outside the borders of California and even outside America. The growing ranks of pro-Chessman forces around the world argued that, even if he was guilty, the punishment he had already suffered was cruel and unusual enough. On the other side were the anti-Chessman forces, including prosecutor Leavy and Judge Fricke, who regularly gave interviews calling him a "vicious, deadly and perverted criminal" who was turning the legal system into a mockery of justice. I might not have used those particular words, but I was certainly with them.

Columbia Pictures bought the movie rights to *Cell 2455*, which gave Chessman more money to pay for more lawyers and provided his enemies with more reasons to want him dead. His next execution date was set: July 30, 1954, the same day that two convicted killers named Jim Wolfe and Joe Johansen were scheduled to die. This gave the authorities at San Quentin some logistical problems. Because there were only two seats in the gas chamber and it took at least two hours to clear the room of lethal gas, they finally decided to send Chessman to his death in the morning and gave the other two an afternoon appointment.

As July 30 got closer and reporters from around the world

gathered at San Quentin, everybody in my office scrambled to find out what Chessman's next move would be so that we could do our best to thwart it. Would he tackle the U.S. Supreme Court again, or try to get another California judge to issue a new stay? When Chessman's chief lawyer, Ben Rice, seemed to disappear a few days before the execution, we were sure he'd gone to Washington. Actually, Rice was hiking through the wilderness of the Trinity Alps in northern Marin County, where Judge Jesse Carter of the California Supreme Court had gone for his vacation. Rice finally found a very surprised Judge Carter camped in a remote area, presented his petition and got Carter to write out a reprieve in longhand, using a tree stump for a desk. Then Rice hurried back to San Quentin, where his client had already been moved from Death Row downstairs to the holding cell, fifteen feet from the gas chamber, in which condemned prisoners spent their last day. It was the closest yet that Chessman had come to the so-called "little green room."

When I heard the news, I immediately called the governor's office and the newspapers and asked for a similar reprieve for Wolfe and Johansen. "There is no reason why a man who can write a book should have an advantage that these two apparently friendless people do not have," I told the press. My motives weren't pure; I was angry at Judge Carter for making what I saw as yet another arbitrary, unilateral decision that delayed the course of justice. Several of his colleagues on the Supreme Court told me privately that they agreed with me, but as a body the court refused to rule on the matter. And not surprisingly, Governor Knight turned down my somewhat ingenuous request for a reprieve, letting Wolfe and Johansen go to their deaths at the time originally reserved for Chessman.

Law enforcers weren't the only ones frustrated by the Chessman case; various newspapers soon took up the refrain. "Reprieves for rapist-kidnapper Caryl Chessman are turning California justice into a light-hearted game of musical chairs with the able assistance of some members of the state judiciary," said an editorial in the *Los Angeles Mirror* headlined "Is There

No End to the Chessman Case?" Other papers in Sacramento, Fresno and San Diego echoed these sentiments. Meanwhile, Chessman's lawyers were off to Washington, petitioning the Supreme Court for the fifth time and setting the stage for the longest delay so far. The high court turned down this latest request for a review, but opened a door by indicating that the federal courts might entertain further motions about the validity of the trial transcript. Back in his cell, Chessman started writing another book, *Trial by Ordeal,* while my office and the state's director of corrections, Richard A. McGee, worked to keep Chessman from getting himself so much attention by refusing to clear any more of his writing for publication. We had the legal right to do this, but again it stirred up a storm of protest.

"When does the wheel stop turning?" asked Federal Judge Louis E. Goodman as he angrily rejected Chessman's new petition for a hearing. "What must the citizen think of our 'nickel in the slot' administration of criminal justice?" Another execution date was set; another judge was found to give Chessman another sixty-day stay; the wheel continued to turn. The U.S. Supreme Court reentered the picture in the summer of 1955, when Justice Tom Clark granted an indefinite stay while the full court considered an appeal. In spite of our best efforts, Chessman managed to finish his second book and smuggled a copy out of San Quentin to his publisher. *Trial by Ordeal* didn't have the same critical or financial success as *Cell 2455, Death Row,* but it earned its author enough to allow him to keep throwing more logs on his legal bonfire.

In October 1955, the U.S. Supreme Court agreed that Chessman's charges should have a hearing in a federal court, and George T. Davis entered the case as one of Chessman's lawyers. Davis was a colorful figure, famous for getting San Francisco union organizer Tom Mooney a pardon in 1939 after he had spent twenty-three years in prison on a trumped-up bomb charge, and for helping German munitions king Alfred Krupp win back some of his fortune after World War II. But even Davis couldn't set off many courtroom fireworks when Judge Goodman—who had made the remarks about "nickel in the slot" criminal justice—

was appointed to run the latest hearing. I sent over two of my best deputies, Arlo Smith and William M. Bennett, to present the state's case when the hearing got under way in San Francisco in January 1956. It lasted ten days, and three days later Judge Goodman once again denied Chessman's request for a new trial.

More petitions were filed and rejected, and judicial tempers continued to flare. When the court of appeals handed down a two-to-one decision against his plea to overturn the Goodman ruling, the dissenting judge released to the press his minority opinion, claiming that Chessman had indeed been denied due process in the matter of the trial transcript. This so angered one of the judges who voted the other way that he attacked his colleague in public, saying that Chessman "had been granted all due process except the long overdue process of his execution." By hastening this along, the judge continued, "the blot on California's juristic escutcheon will be, if not wholly erased, at least partly dimmed."

Despite the state's best efforts to stop him, we discovered that Chessman had been busy writing his third book, *The Face of Justice*. Since his cell was now regularly searched and all his notebooks and papers examined, Chessman cleverly wrote this book in ink on the backs of sheets of carbon paper which he left in plain sight. Then the finished manuscript was again smuggled out of San Quentin, probably in a garbage can with the help of another prisoner and possibly one of his lawyers, and was sent off to be published. Also in the pipeline was yet another petition to the U.S. Supreme Court, asking for a complete review of the case. Meanwhile, George Davis took time out to help keep another client, Burton Abbott, from the gas chamber. When that case came to an abrupt end on March 15, 1957, after the episode of the aircraft carrier and late phone call from Governor Knight's secretary, I issued my plea to the legislature to consider a five-year moratorium on the death penalty. The Abbott case may have been the immediate reason for my request, but living on the Chessman roller coaster for the last seven years was also a large part of my motivation.

By a surprising vote of five to three, the U.S. Supreme Court ruled in June 1957 that what Chessman had been saying all those years was probably true, that he "has never had his day in court on the controversial issues of fact and law involved in the settlement of the record on which his conviction was affirmed." The high court ordered a full hearing on the issue of the trial transcript. Also surprising was the fact that Justice William O. Douglas, famous as a foe of capital punishment, wrote the dissenting opinion. "The conclusion is irresistible that Chessman is playing a game with the courts, stalling for time while the facts in the case grow cold," Douglas wrote.

Caryl Chessman's "day in court"—seventy-five days, in fact— got under way in Los Angeles on November 25, 1957. The local newspapers had just been filled with stories of another trial, also prosecuted by J. Miller Leavy: that of a painting contractor named Edward Simon Wein, who was being called the "Want Ad Rapist" because of his method of answering ads offering items for sale, then attacking women who were alone in the house. Leavy told the jury that Wein "made Chessman look like a schoolboy," and they believed him: he was convicted of five separate violations of Section 209 and received five death penalties, even though none of his victims had died. In the years to come, Edward Simon Wein would also play a large part in my own life.

Even though a new judge, Walter R. Evans, replaced a seriously ill Judge Fricke at the lengthy Los Angeles hearing; even though Chessman and his lawyers fired all their best shots against the tainted trial transcript and the court reporter who produced it; and even though the world press covered the story in detail, in the end nothing was changed. In February 1958, while the California Republicans fought among themselves and I began to think seriously of running for governor, Judge Evans rejected every request that the defense had made. Soon Caryl Chessman was back in his cell at San Quentin, busy filing the appeals that would keep him alive until I took office and he became my personal problem.

* * *

Those appeals and other delays kept me from having to make any decisions about Chessman for most of my first year as governor. And what a great first year it was, as even my political enemies were forced to admit. A sweeping water resources development program which California needed desperately was finally in place; a new fair employment practices act was protecting everyone's right to work; a plan to revamp the state's higher education system had been drafted; the budget was well on its way to being balanced; a state economic development commission and a consumers' council had been established; other newly enacted measures covered city traffic and smog, old-age and mental health issues. Thanks to a supportive state legislature, thirty-five of the forty major proposals that we sent to them had been enacted into law. Newspapers were already putting me up there with the two previous California governors I admired most, Earl Warren and Hiram Johnson, and there was even some talk about me as a dark-horse candidate for president in the 1960 election. I loved every minute of it.

During that first year, I commuted the sentences of three other condemned prisoners in addition to John Crooker. Two of them—Edward Simon Wein, the "Want Ad Rapist," and Charles Evan Turville, Jr.—I'll discuss in detail in subsequent chapters. The third was Harold Almus Langdon, who struck and injured a girl while attempting to rape her, and had been sentenced to death—like Chessman and Wein—under Section 209. I commuted his sentence to life without possibility of parole because no robbery was involved.

In that first year, I also denied clemency to six other men sentenced to death. After carefully examining each case, I could find no legal or moral reason to go against the judgment of the court. The prisoners went to their deaths in the gas chamber, and my daughter Kathleen, who was a teenager at the time, remembers the Thursday nights before their executions as being very tense times around the house.

In October 1959, facing his seventh execution date, Chessman requested and was granted a clemency hearing. In his typical fashion, the request came in the form of a long and tendentious letter from him to clemency secretary Cecil Poole, dated October 6, 1959:

Dear Mr. Poole:

Dated September 30, 1959, I received the following communication from "F. R. Dickson, Warden, by: L. S. Nelson, Associate Warden in Charge:

"At 10:30 A.M. this date I received a call from Mr. Cecil Poole, clemency secretary to Governor Edmund G. Brown. Mr. Poole stated that if you, or your attorneys, want consideration for executive clemency from the Governor, it will be necessary for you, or them, to make application for such. This application must be in the hands of the Governor by October 9, 1959; otherwise, no executive clemency will be considered.

"Mr. Poole stated that no particular form of application need be followed but that this must be in writing. The Governor is not interested in side issues of a lie detector test, the use of sodium amythol (sic) etc. Your application must pertain only to the issue of executive clemency.

"Your attention is again directed to the deadline of October 9, 1959."

With a growing sense of shock and disbelief, I have read and reread this communication. It is apparent that the Governor, through you, Mr. Poole, has not extended a genuine opportunity for me to apply for executive clemency but has delivered a coercive ultimatum. Evidently, by necessary implication, innocence has become a side issue. Evidently also, by the terms of your ultimatum, you are telling me that I only can ask for clemency if, in effect, I admit guilt and approach the throne crying out "Unclean!" and begging for mercy. Since I do not happen to be guilty of these so-called Red Light Bandit crimes, I angrily reject the conditions under which our good Governor might deign to consider an application from me.

I think it is a terrible thing when, after I have spent more than 11 years in a death cell, often literally having come within hours and minutes of being put to death, all the while maintaining innocence and asking only a meaningful opportunity to prove it, this state's Chief Executive would resort to using his clemency powers in such a markedly coercive way. California must indeed be desperate to "vindicate" itself and its treatment of me when its Governor, in language thinly veiled, endeavors to force a false confession of guilt as the price I must pay for consideration for clemency.

Further, both you and the Governor know full well the case still is pending and being actively litigated in the courts, and thus, by arbitrarily setting a deadline, you are telling me in effect that I must choose between taking the case to the Supreme Court of the United States and asking for clemency, since there isn't time to prepare competent applications for both. I object strenuously to being compelled to make such a choice, yet since it has been forced upon me I must tell you frankly that I choose the Supreme Court. And I reject your arbitrary deadline, Mr. Poole. At the same time I suggest both you and the Governor turn to your dictionary and reread the definition of clemency. And you might also look at humanity. And justice.

As Attorney General, Mr. Brown took occasion to make a great many speeches taking a fearless if not always too rational stand against the "mocker of justice" Caryl Chessman. If he has forgotten what he has said, I have a thick file of newspaper clippings and some tape recordings he will find instructive. Now, in the light of this ultimatum from you, Mr. Poole, I wonder if Mr. Brown has not brought his politically advantageous prejudices with him to the Governor's chair. Will you kindly ask the Governor and then inform me in writing if he does not consider himself wholly disqualified from acting on the case and determining whether I am entitled to clemency by all the proper means at his command? I believe this communication—that is, your communication, which I assume had his blessing—reveals such a fixed and continuing bias that his thinking on the matter is hopelessly colored and tainted. My point is this: If the Governor believes it to be to his political advantage to slay, so be it. But let him step aside and permit the Lieutenant Governor to determine the clemency question on its merits. In short, the mob may applaud treating me so arbitrarily and arrogantly; history won't. But then, history can't vote.

Yours very truly,
Caryl Chessman

With that rhetoric out of his system, at least momentarily, Chessman let his lawyers make the formal application for clemency. He happened to be right about political implications, even though he used verbal overkill to impugn my motives. From the many hours of discussion we'd already had on the subject, I knew that the key members of my staff—Poole plus Executive Secretary Fred Dutton and Press Secretary Hale Champion—not only believed Chessman to be guilty, as I did, but were convinced that any weakness on my part in enforcing the law of the state could be extremely dangerous to what we all hoped to achieve. There was also a serious legal roadblock in my way: because Chessman had several prior felony convictions, the state constitution prohibited me from granting any sort of commutation without the written approval of a majority of the California Supreme Court. Both Poole and I privately sounded out Chief Justice Phil Gibson, who told us that there were only three pro-Chessman votes on the seven-man court.

Despite all this, I went into the clemency hearing with a prejudice toward finding a way to spare Chessman's life. How else can I explain a comment I made during the hearing to J. Miller Leavy, who had come up from Los Angeles to testify against Chessman? "Don't you think the prosecution should be satisfied with eleven and a half years on Death Row for this man?" I asked Leavy. "Or do you insist on your Roman holiday next Friday?" Leavy looked surprised for a moment, then recovered himself and continued his argument.

At the end of the hearing, crowded with reporters from as far away as Sweden and Brazil, I said that I intended to do a lot of thinking and praying over the weekend, and that my decision would be announced on Monday. I was departing Sunday night for a governors' conference and a meeting in Chicago with presidential candidate Adlai Stevenson, so I sat down with Poole and Champion over the weekend to thrash out a decision and a statement. My secretaries were both adamant about the fact that nothing new had been raised during the hearing, that the chief issue of the trial transcript had been rejected by many courts. I agreed, but pointed out how impressed I had been by the strong support given to Chessman's plea for clemency by four Los Angeles newspaper reporters who had covered the recent seventy-five-day hearing. All had begun the hearing unsympathetic to Chessman; all had come away from it convinced that his life should be spared. They countered this with medical testimony about the precarious mental condition of one of Chessman's victims, still confined to a state hospital. Never once during his years on Death Row had Chessman ever expressed any contrition or sympathy for her or his other victims. I was also reminded that the California Supreme Court would not give me a majority vote on commutation. In the end, I agreed that Chessman's request for clemency should be denied. Poole and Champion drafted a statement to that effect, and I approved it. On Sunday, just before I left for Chicago, I changed the language somewhat. On Monday morning, I called from Chicago and asked to change some of the wording a bit more. Cecil told me that the press was already outside, waiting for the statement. "Let it go," I said to him.

"Caryl Chessman has not sought executive clemency from me. To the contrary, he has declared that he seeks only vindication. This I cannot give him. The evidence of his guilt is overwhelming," the statement began.

"Despite his disavowal of an interest in clemency, I have on my own initiative very carefully examined every phase of the voluminous record in this case. And, at the request of his attorneys, I conducted an extensive personal hearing on October 15. The record shows a deliberate career of robberies and kidnappings, followed by sexual assaults and acts of perversion, accomplished at the point of a loaded gun. . . .

"The courts have inquired into every aspect of his trial. They have upheld his conviction by a jury as fair and legal. No case in modern history has received more careful scrutiny by both state and federal judiciary. It is a tribute to the American judicial system that so much concern has been shown—and properly shown—for the rights of an individual. The Governor is duty bound to accept the considered judgements of the courts as to Chessman's guilt and the fairness of his trial as final.

"My own personal feelings with respect to capital punishment are well known. I am opposed to it. Yet the Legislature has repeatedly considered the question of whether the death penalty should remain the policy of this State, and has decided that it should. . . .

"I repeat and emphasize my own opposition to capital punishment, whether a life has been taken or not. But I have sworn to uphold and faithfully to execute the laws of this State. Capital punishment remains part of those laws, and the Chief Executive, whatever his personal beliefs, must respect and be guided by the will of the people, expressed by their elected representatives and enacted into the statutes.

"The clemency power conferred on the Governor by our State Constitution is great. But it is an extraordinary power, to be exercised only when justified by compelling circumstances. I have searched the record, and my conscience, for some sufficient basis for resolving this issue in favor of clemency. I have been unable to do so. I have used the power of clemency before, and in proper cases I will use it again. I do not believe this is a proper case.

"Many thoughtful people have communicated their sentiments to me in this matter. I am deeply grateful for their expressions. But in the final instance, the Governor alone, guided by the Constitution and the law, must make the decision. His is the power. His is the responsibility.

"The established findings of this case—a deliberate plan of robberies, sexual attacks and the use of a loaded gun—have weighed heavily in my thinking. So too has Chessman's failure to show contrition. His attitude has been one of steadfast arrogance and contempt for society and its laws. I have considered too the matter of prior felony convictions. Our Constitution recognizes this as a factor in clemency, and limits the Governor's power to act except upon recommendation from the State Supreme Court where there is a prior felony conviction.

"Because of all these considerations, I have decided that I will not intervene in the case of Caryl Chessman."

*   *   *

36

Forty-eight hours before his October execution date, Chessman was granted a stay by Justice William O. Douglas while the rest of the U.S. Supreme Court considered his latest request for a review. In December, that court turned down the request without comment, and a new execution date of February 19, 1960, was set. During this period, the public clamor surrounding the case expanded in size and volume. Eleanor Roosevelt, Aldous Huxley, Ray Bradbury, Steve Allen and Bishop James Pike were only a few of the well-known people who wrote or called me to ask for clemency. Groups of all kinds—ethnic, religious, educational, anti–capital-punishment—marched regularly in San Francisco's Union Square and outside the gates of San Quentin. But while most of the demonstrations were pro-Chessman, the thousands of letters and postcards that poured into my office were almost evenly split, showing just how divisive the issue was. Some of the anti-Chessman mail was illiterate and insane, but a lot of it came from sensible, concerned people who worried about the long-term effects on our justice system if he were allowed to evade the death penalty.

Claiming that Chessman's eleven and a half years on Death Row constituted cruel and unusual punishment in violation of the Eighth Amendment to the Constitution, George Davis asked Judge Goodman for a new hearing. On January 28, 1960, Goodman turned down the petition but for the first time showed some wavering in his attitude. He called me privately before he announced his ruling, saying he had no choice except to deny but that he thought I would be acting properly if I commuted. "I'll take that part out of my ruling if it makes it more difficult for you," he said. I thanked him for his tact, but told him that nothing he or anyone else said could make my job any less difficult. "I would suggest that the California Supreme Court or Governor Brown strongly consider clemency in this case," Goodman's ruling said.

Reporters caught up with me on a trip to Santa Barbara and asked for my comment on Judge Goodman's suggestion. "When a judge of his stature publicly states there is a basis for judicial review, I certainly wouldn't cast that opinion aside," I answered, managing to sound surprised. But I wondered to myself if Judge Goodman didn't know as well as I did that the Supreme Court vote was stacked against any such action.

In February, a week before the latest execution date, Judge Richard Chambers of the Ninth Circuit Court of Appeals seemed to slam the door on the Chessman case for good when he rejected all the points raised in a new petition and blasted Judge Goodman for his comments. "I do not see how we can offer life as a prize for one who can stall the legal processes for a given number of years," he said. On the question of cruel and unusual punishment, Judge Chambers continued, "We are told of his agonies on Death Row. True, it would be hell for most people. But here is no ordinary man. I think he has heckled his keeper long enough."

In truth, and in retrospect, I think it was this aspect of Chessman's personality—this perceived "heckling of his keeper"—that turned off the compassion I might otherwise have felt for him, the compassion I did feel and act on for other condemned prisoners. Over the last few months, I had made strong public statements in support of proposed moratoriums on the death penalty. Yet I seemed to be able to live with the idea of Chessman being put to death as something completely separate from the concept of capital punishment. Chessman himself probably said it best, in a statement he made on February 18. Asked by a reporter if he thought that commuting his sentence would make it harder to win passage of my latest antideath penalty bill, Chessman replied, "It might be that if I were the governor, I would let myself die to bring about the abolition of capital punishment."

The 1960 Winter Olympics were to open at Squaw Valley on February 18; I was supposed to attend, but because of the Chessman execution I bowed out and persuaded Fred Dutton to go along with my wife Bernice and our youngest daughter, Kathleen. Bernice didn't want to leave me alone in the Governor's Mansion; she was fully aware of my complicated feelings about Chessman, but agreed with Dutton and my other staff members that I had no right to grant a reprieve. A loving wife and mother, she was still the tough-minded daughter of a San Francisco police captain and had no sympathy for Chessman. "You have all these people depending on you," she reminded me before she left, talking not only about my staff but about the people I had been elected to serve. "You simply cannot ignore them and destroy your effectiveness as governor because of one man who is no good anyway."

Similar worries about my wavering were no doubt what prompted Hale Champion, Cecil Poole and several other members of my staff to make sure that I spent as little time alone as possible on the evening of February 18. We had a long and argumentative dinner at the Mansion Inn, and when they finally left me to walk across the street to the Governor's Mansion by myself, we were agreed that I would do nothing to halt the execution. To that end, I had all the telephones disconnected except for one private line. Champion and Poole went back to the office to handle one last document from Chessman's lawyers, and I settled in to catch up on some reading. The phone rang occasionally, friends or members of the press who had my private number, and to them all I said there was nothing more I could or would do for Chessman.

Then, about 9 P.M., my son Jerry called from the University of California campus at Berkeley. He had just left the Jesuit order in Los Gatos after three and a half years, and was now planning to become a lawyer. Jerry's decision to study for the priesthood had stirred up some strong emotions in our family: Bernice used to cry on the way home from our monthly visits to him. My own feelings were a mixture of great pride in the strength of his convictions and the inevitable sadness caused by an only son choosing this particular road. During his years with the Jesuits, we had many discussions about the moral aspects of political choices. Now he was calling to urge me to give Chessman a reprieve. "Son," I told him, "there's nothing I can do. I need the consent of the Supreme Court to commute, and Phil Gibson has already told me that not only will they vote four to three against me, but they'll write a majority opinion kicking me in the teeth."

Jerry listened to that argument, then said, "Dad, can't you give him a sixty-day stay and go to the legislature to ask for a moratorium on the death penalty?"

"There isn't one chance in a thousand that the legislature will vote for a moratorium," I told him. "They've turned down the last eight in a row."

Then Jerry said, "But Dad, if you were a doctor and there was one chance in a thousand of saving a patient's life, wouldn't you take it?"

I thought about that for a moment. "You're right," I finally said. "I'll do it."

"Will you really?" Jerry asked, surprised that he had convinced me so quickly and easily. But he was plowing very fertile ground; I had been searching my soul for an excuse to do something. I called the office, where Poole was reading a last-minute request from Chessman's lawyers for a delay. "I'm thinking of giving him a sixty-day stay and calling for a special session of the legislature to vote on a moratorium," I told Cecil. "I think we tried that before and it didn't work," Poole answered in a neutral voice, because Chessman lawyer Rosalie Asher was still sitting across from him. "Well, I'm going to do it," I said. "I've got something to show you," said Poole. "I'll bring it right over." "You'd better make it fast," I told him as I hung up.

What Cecil had to show me was one of the thousands of telegrams that had been pouring in to our office in the last few days, still being logged in by secretaries at that hour of the night. This particular one was from Roy Rubottom, Jr., assistant secretary of state, who warned that the growing world hysteria surrounding Chessman's execution might ignite hostile demonstrations and endanger President Eisenhower's upcoming visit to Montevideo, Uruguay. It provided me with the public excuse I needed to justify my decision to give Chessman a stay, and in the days ahead I mentioned the telegram often but played down my conversation with Jerry.

Poole and Champion raced back to the mansion with the telegram, still convinced that a stay was a bad idea. We argued back and forth for several minutes. Then the phone rang, and both

Cecil and Hale ran to answer it. "You guys are too tough," I told them. "*I'll* answer it!" It was a reporter from Los Angeles, calling to see if I had changed my mind. "I'll have a statement for you in about an hour," I told him. Then I called San Quentin. Warden Fred Dickson was having a last visit with Chessman, who had already been moved down to the holding cell next to the gas chamber when I called. "You can send him back upstairs," I told Dickson. "I'm giving him a sixty-day reprieve."

Champion, Poole and I quickly put our heads together and came up with a statement, issued over my signature: "I have determined to reprieve Caryl Chessman for 60 days. I do this because I want to give the people of California an opportunity, through the legislature, to express themselves once more on capital punishment. During this 60 days, I will put the issue on a special call concurrent with the legislature's budget session.

"The people of California are clearly divided on this basic issue. The thousands of communications I have received in this case have centered not so much on the person of Caryl Chessman and his history as on whether this State should continue capital punishment. If the people, acting through their elected representatives, determine that the present law shall be continued in effect, Caryl Chessman will be executed under the law.

"Three of the seven justices of the State Supreme Court have recommended clemency, and the Federal District Court judge who has had most to do with this case has indicated a similar position. I do not know all of their reasons. But it has been demonstrated to me that there is a basic division among us.

"I believe that the legislature, representing all the people of California, should have the opportunity during the next 60 days to speak for them. I hope the legislature will abolish capital punishment, but I, of course, will abide by its decision, whatever that decision may be."

"It will really hit the fan now," said Jack Welter of the *San Francisco Chronicle* when he heard that I'd given Chessman a stay. And he was right. Only someone who lived through it can fully appreciate the heightened emotions of that period. The violence and anger of the anti-Chessman movement, as vocal as the other side if not as highly visible or as well-organized, now had a new target—Pat Brown. The volume of mail pouring into my office increased, with attacks on me as common as abuse of Chessman and the legal system. Dummies of me were hung in effigy in Modesto, Long Beach and West Los Angeles. Members of my own party accused me of weakness, cowardice and passing the buck to the state legislature. Even newspapers like the *Sacramento Bee,* which had always been a strong and loyal supporter, turned against me on this issue. At the opening of the Hollywood Park racetrack a few days after the stay was announced, Bernice went down to put the wreath on the winning horse while I stayed in the stands. When the name "Mrs. Pat Brown" was announced, there was a loud chorus of booing; rage and shame almost made me run for the door. I was booed again at Squaw Valley when the Winter Olympics ended, and at the opening of Candlestick Park in San Francisco while Vice President Nixon looked on. One state assemblyman announced that he was starting a recall movement to remove me from office.

While a part of me reacted with regret and bewilderment to this sudden change in public attitude, making me think seriously of withdrawing from public life, another part was determined to mount as strong a fight as possible before the legislature in support of a moratorium on the death penalty. Champion and Poole, putting aside their personal feelings about Chessman, talked to members of the fifteen-person Judiciary Committee, where the decision would be made to call for a floor vote; they came away thinking we at least had a chance. We brought in experts from all over the world and drafted the address that I delivered to the legislature on March 2. I include it in full here because I think it spells out exactly how I felt about the death penalty at the time.

"As an act of public conscience from the experience of over a decade and a half in law enforcement work, I ask the legislature to abolish the death penalty in California. There are powerful and compelling reasons why this should be done. It is not based on maudlin sympathy for the criminal and depraved. And although I believe the death penalty constitutes an affront to human dignity and brutalizes and degrades society, I do not merely for these reasons urge this course for our state.

"I have reached this momentous resolution after sixteen years of careful, intimate and personal experience with the application of the death penalty in this state. This experience embraces seven years as district attorney of San Francisco, eight years as attorney general of this state, and now fourteen months as Governor. I have had a day-to-day, first-hand familiarity with crime and punishment surpassed by very few.

"Society has both the right and the moral duty to protect itself against its enemies. This natural and prehistoric axiom has never successfully been refuted. If by ordered death society is really protected and our homes and institutions guarded, then even the most extreme of all penalties can be justified.

"But the naked, simple fact is that the death penalty has been a gross failure. Beyond its horror and incivility, it has neither protected the innocent nor deterred the wicked. The recurrent spectacle of publicly sanctioned killing has cheapened human life and dignity without the redeeming grace which comes from justice meted out swiftly, evenly, humanely.

"The death penalty is invoked too randomly, too irregularly, too unpredictably and too tardily to be defended as an effective example warning away wrongdoers.

"In California, for example, in 1955 there were 417 homicides. But only fifty-two defendants were convicted of first degree murder. And only 8, or 2 percent, were in fact sentenced to death. There can be no meaningful exemplary value in a punishment the incidence of which is but one in fifty.

"Nor is the death penalty to be explained as society's ultimate weapon of desperation against the unregenerate and perverse. The study of executions over a fifteen-year-period produces the startling facts that of 110 condemned cases, 49 percent of those executed had never suffered a prior felony conviction; that 75 percent of them came from families which had been broken by divorce, separation or otherwise when the condemned was still in his teens.

"Again I say that if this most drastic of sanctions could be said substantially to serve the ends of legal justice by adding to our safety and security, it would deserve some greater place in our respect. But no available data from any place or time that I have been able to find from research over many years gives support to the grand argument that the presence or absence of the death penalty exerts any substantial effect upon the incidence of homicide.

"Specifically, the death penalty has been abolished in nine states (Minnesota, Wisconsin, Michigan, Rhode Island, North Dakota, Maine, Alaska and Hawaii) as well as in Puerto Rico and in twenty-nine foreign countries (Sweden, Belgium, Norway, Italy, West Germany, Austria and twenty-two others).

"In none of these states has the homicide rate increased, and indeed in comparison with other states their rates seem somewhat lower. And these rates are lower not because of the absence of the death penalty but because of particular social organization, composition of population, economic and political conditions.

"I have attached to this document a map of the United States in which the various states are shaded to indicate their murder rate over a ten-year period from 1948 through 1957, compiled by the California Department of Corrections. It shows graphically that the states without capital punishment along with several other states which do retain the death penalty have the least incidence of homicides. And in striking contrast, twelve southern states, all zealously applying the death penalty, have the highest homicide rate.

"This last fact points up the most glaring weakness of all, that no matter how efficient and fair the death penalty may seem in theory, in actual practice in California as elsewhere it is primarily inflicted upon the weak, the poor, the ignorant, and against racial minorities. In California, and in the nation as a whole, the overwhelming majority of those executed are psychotic or near-psychotic, alcoholic, mentally defective or otherwise demonstrably mentally unstable. In the experience of former Wardens Lewis Lawes of Sing Sing and Clinton P. Duffy of San Quentin, seldom are those with funds or prestige convicted of capital offenses, and even more seldom are they executed.

"As shocking as may be the statistics in our Deep South where the most extensive use of the death penalty is made against the most defenseless and downtrodden of the population, the Negroes, let it be remembered too that in California, in the fifteen-year-period ending in 1953, covering 110 executions, 30 percent were Mexicans and Negroes, more than double the combined population percentages of these two groups at the time. Indeed, only last year, 1959, out of forty-eight executions in the United States, twenty-one only were whites, while twenty-seven were Negroes. I believe you will find these figures compelling evidence of the gross unfairness and social injustice which has characterized the application of the death penalty.

"And finally I bring to your attention the lessons I have learned here, in California, in sixteen years of public service but especially since I became Governor. Last January I inaugurated the practice of personally conducting executive clemency hearings in every death case upon request. Each such case is carefully investigated and comes to me complete with transcripts, investigative reports and up-to-date psychological, neuropsychiatric and sociological evaluations.

"These are all hard cases to review and consider. There have been nineteen of them these past fourteen months. They present a dreary procession of sordid, senseless violence, perpetrated by the wandering outcasts of the state. Not a single one of these nineteen accomplished a pittance of material gain. Nine of the nineteen suffered obvious and deep mental imbalance. In the only three cases where actual murder was entertained by conscious design, sickness of mind was clinically established to have existed for many years. All of them were products of the hinterlands of social, economic and educational disadvantage.

"Six of these I have commuted to life imprisonment without

45

possibility of parole. Eight of them we have given unto the executioner: miserable, bewildered sacrifices. We have taken their lives. But I have seen in the files and transcripts, in the books which we have now closed upon them, that who they were and what they were played just as big a part in their ultimate condemnation as what they did. And I saw also that, but for just the slightest twist of circumstances, those eight might have received a term of years as did the other 98 percent of those who killed.

"I have studied their cases and I know that not a single execution has ever halted the sale of a single gun or restrained a moment's blind rage.

"And in these cases, too, there looms always the ugly chance that innocent men may be condemned, however careful are our courts and juries. Our judicial system gives us pride, but tempered by the realization that mankind is subject to error.

"And this to me has been no idle fear. Within six months after I became Governor there came to me the duty to pardon a man who had, despite the care of court and counsel of his choice, been convicted of the willful slaying of his wife.

"This man, John Henry Fry by name, admittedly under the influence of alcohol at the time of the crime, stood convicted by the force of circumstances which he could not explain. Happily, he was not executed. And last June 16th we pardoned him for that which he had never done.

"Here but for the grace of God there might now be on our hands the blood of a man poor, ignorant, friendless—and innocent.

"I issue this call for consideration of the death penalty as a matter of conviction and conscience.

"I believe the entire history of our civilization is a struggle to bring about a greater measure of humanity, compassion and dignity among us. I believe those qualities will be the greater when the action proposed here is achieved—and not just for the wretches whose execution is changed to life imprisonment, but for each of us."

*　*　*

We wouldn't have to wait long for the legislature to act: a hearing on the death-penalty moratorium was scheduled for March 9. One newspaper commented that "the Governor is bearing a burden few will help him carry in the stormy days ahead," and almost immediately that prediction began to come true. Faced with a primary election in June, even loyal Democrats who had previously voted against the death penalty were now quoted as saying they resented the issue being turned into a "political football." Although a motion had been passed not to mention the Chessman case during the hearing, many people felt the pressure of the constant headlines. "I think the Chessman problem is a very unfair implication and responsibility to place on the members of the legislature," one formerly anti–capital-punishment assemblywoman said.

The hearing began at 9 A.M. and continued past midnight. The last witness called was Los Angeles prosecutor J. Miller Leavy. He wasn't here this time to continue his personal war against Chessman, at least not directly: he had some startling revelations about another famous California death-penalty case. Convicted murderer Barbara Graham had gone to her death in the gas chamber in 1955 proclaiming her innocence, and a subsequent book and film about her, called *I Want to Live!* seemed to support that claim. Now Leavy wanted to tell the world that on his deathbed this past June former San Quentin Warden Harley Teets had revealed that Graham had actually confessed her guilt to him before she was executed. "Is this the first time this has been made public, here tonight?" asked a surprised state Senator Fred Farr, one of the sponsors of the moratorium. "Yes," Leavy answered. "I had thought I would make it public sometime."

"He made it public because I asked him to!" interrupted state Senator Edward Regan, chairman of the Judiciary Committee, who then called for a vote on the proposed moratorium. Stunned by the Leavy testimony, which was later doubted and denied by experts including Erle Stanley Gardner, the committee voted eight to seven against this latest moratorium. The death penalty was again confirmed as the law of the State of California for the ninth time in ten years.

The next morning I made this statement: "I am, of course, deeply sorry that the bill banning the death penalty in California did not receive the necessary eight votes in the Senate Judiciary Committee to permit further consideration on the Senate floor. I am told that the presentation of the case for abolition was the most impressive ever made in California, and I am sure it will have played an important long-term role when capital punishment is finally abolished in California, as it inevitably will be.

"I am informed that the issue is now resolved, and that the legislature intends to adjourn the special session relating to the death penalty. As I have said before, such action is a legislative prerogative which I must and will respect. If the legislature adjourns the death penalty call today, the regular schedule of executions will continue under the Constitution and laws of the State of California.

"I have heard it said, and I have read in the newspapers, that this action of the legislature leaves the fate of Caryl Chessman in my hands. This is not true. I continue to have the general power of clemency. But because Chessman has been convicted of other felonies, I could exercise clemency—as distinguished from a brief reprieve—only on the affirmative recommendation of the State Supreme Court. The Court has twice refused such a recommendation. The reasons for the reprieve I granted last month no longer exist. Constitutionally I am therefore now absolutely powerless to act again in that case."

Meanwhile, a judge in Los Angeles had set a ninth execution date for Caryl Chessman—May 2, 1960, a Monday, the first time in living memory that a day other than the traditional Friday had been chosen. As the days ticked away, Milton Machlin and William Read Woodfield, two writers from *Argosy*, a men's magazine in New York that had a popular "Court of Last Resort" feature, worked hard to turn up convincing evidence that someone other than Chessman had committed the "red-light" crimes. Their candidate was another small-time criminal named Charles Terranova, whose physical description generally matched Chessman's. But they were hampered most of all by Chessman's persistent refusal to give them solid facts rather than coy hints to go on. Attorney General Stanley Mosk, several federal judges, Cecil Poole and I all looked over their material and found nothing to change our minds about Chessman's guilt.

As more than two hundred letters and telegrams a day continued to arrive at my office—90 percent of them now urging me to act to save Chessman's life—I once again consulted privately with Chief Justice Phil Gibson of the California Supreme Court to see if the balance against commutation had shifted. The vote was still four to three, Gibson told me, with one justice even postponing his planned retirement so that he could continue to vote against Chessman. Learning about this, some reporters suggested that I grant Chessman another sixty- or ninety-day stay, so that this particular justice could retire and be replaced by someone more lenient. I replied that I thought this "would be an unwarranted executive attempt to exercise influence on the judiciary."

In Sausalito, across the San Francisco Bay from San Quentin, a giant torch was lit on a hillside to burn until Chessman was reprieved or executed. Former madam Sally Stanford, long a supporter of mine and now a legitimate restaurant owner, was one of its sponsors. World figures as diverse as Albert Schweitzer and Brigitte Bardot sent telegrams asking for mercy for Chessman. And on the night of May 1, hundreds of protesters, including celebrities such as Marlon Brando and Shirley MacLaine, camped out on the lawn of the Governor's Mansion in Sacramento. As television cameras rolled and flashbulbs popped, I went out to talk with these sincere people, trying in that mild spring night air to make them understand that there was nothing more I could do.

Was I being completely honest with them? Couldn't I have given Chessman another stay? The truth is that the reaction to my last stay was so much more violent and angry than I had expected that I never seriously considered granting another one—especially with the State Supreme Court still against commutation. The unanimous feeling among my staff was that the February stay was a stupid, foolish, wasteful and dangerous thing for me to have done. If I tried to give Chessman another stay, I could have been charged with exceeding my powers under the California constitution, adding fuel to the recall fire. And there was one other point, something which one of Chessman's lawyers tried to capitalize on in an appeal: by granting him a stay in February, hadn't I in a sense been guilty of cruelty to Chessman, giving him false hope in a situation where I knew none really existed?

On the morning of May 2, the State Supreme Court convened at 8 A.M., two hours before the scheduled execution time, to hear an appeal from Davis and Asher based on information gathered by the writers from *Argosy* magazine. At 9:15, a clerk told the waiting lawyers that the court had denied their writ by a vote of four to three. Davis and Asher then ran to a waiting car and drove to the Federal Court House, where Judge Goodman was ready to hear another last-minute plea. Reporters on the steps delayed the lawyers for a minute; a slow elevator took up more time; so it was 10 A.M. when Judge Goodman looked up from the papers just handed to him and said, "I will grant you at least a thirty-minute stay while I study this." He asked his secretary to dial the prison; there was another delay when she first dialed a wrong number. . . .

I had been in my office in Sacramento since before 8 A.M. Just outside my door, Cecil Poole manned the special open line to San Quentin that we used on execution days. Ever since the Burton Abbott fiasco, we had made an informal arrangement with the warden to delay the actual dropping of the pellets for four or five minutes after the appointed hour. At about 9:40, Cecil reported that he heard a sound "like a thousand toilets flushing," which was the sealing with water of the vents of the gas chamber. Then, at about 10:05, the assistant warden told Poole that the pellets had been dropped and that the execution couldn't be stopped.

Cecil relayed the message to me; I got up from my desk and headed for my car, where my Highway Patrol driver was waiting to drive me to Folsom Lake, a quiet place about fifty miles away. There was a phone in the car in case I had to be reached, but at that moment I wanted to be as alone with my thoughts as any governor could be.

It was less than a minute after my departure, I learned later, when Cecil heard another phone ringing on the open line to San Quentin. It was Judge Goodman, whose voice he recognized, asking if the execution had begun yet, because he wanted to give Chessman a thirty-minute stay while he read the petition just delivered to him. The assistant warden told him it was too far along to stop. Chessman was officially declared dead at 10:12 A.M.

Later that day, in reply to hundreds of requests for my thoughts, I issued this brief statement: "I regret equally every execution in California, past and future, including the one today. My personal opposition to capital punishment remains as strong as ever. I continue to hope that the people of California will change the law. Until they do, however, I must continue to uphold the law and the provisions of the Constitution with all the strength at my command.

"My oath of office takes precedence over all else in my public life and actions. It has always done so in the past; it will always do so in the future."

World reaction against the execution was predictably strong: crowds attacked U.S. embassies in Lisbon, Stockholm, Montevideo and dozens of other cities in Europe and South America. And if I expected my life at home to be any easier with Chessman dead, I was soon proved wrong. In July, when I led the California delegation to the Democratic National Convention, I was booed as my name was placed in nomination as a favorite son. That wonderful legislative honeymoon mood of my first year was definitely over: even some Democrats who had been staunch supporters now saw me as weak and vacillating. By December 1961,

I was so far behind Nixon in the polls that I flew to Washington to consult with California senators and congressmen. I offered to withdraw from the 1962 election if a stronger candidate could be found, but nobody else wanted to give up a safe seat for what they saw as a definite kamikaze mission.

Fallout from the Chessman case continued to increase during the 1962 election campaign. Sensing weakness, Richard Nixon—a strong supporter of capital punishment—used the issue to attack me whenever he could. At one televised debate, he deviated from the set format to say, "You're not in favor of killing *any* criminals, are you, Governor Brown?" To which I replied in anger, "And you believe in gassing pickpockets, don't you?" In the end, despite the polls, I beat Nixon by 200,000 votes and was reelected governor for another four years. But the shadow of the gas chamber, and of Caryl Chessman, hung over my last years. And when Ronald Reagan defeated me by almost a million votes in 1966, the same issue and its surrounding aura of weakness and vacillation had a lot to do with it.

Human beings learn from all kinds of experiences, particularly from ones as traumatic as the Chessman case. Twenty-eight years after his death, what can I say that I have learned? Chessman was a nasty, arrogant, unrepentant man, almost certainly guilty of the crimes he was convicted of, but I didn't think those crimes deserved the death penalty then, and I certainly don't think so now. And his trial was so badly tainted by that faulty transcript that his sentence should have been commuted by *someone* to life without possibility of parole. By the time I became the someone with that power, other people—myself included as attorney general—had successfully stoked the fires of public indignation so high against him for "heckling his keeper" that such action was virtually impossible, especially for an elected official with a responsibility to his constituency and the programs he hoped to implement for the common good. I firmly believe all of that. I also believe that I should have found a way to spare Chessman's life.

CHAPTER THREE

The Soldier

The State of California had spent twelve years and over $30,000 curing Erwin ("Machine Gun") Walker of mental illness; now it wanted me to do my job and send him to the gas chamber. Just a few months before, the Chessman case had almost destroyed my career. How could I hope to survive, let alone continue to make progress, if I even considered commuting the death sentence of this convicted cop killer?

I've always had good relations with the police, starting with my father-in-law, Captain Arthur Layne, who had a reputation for honesty in a San Francisco Police Department that was often charged with corruption. We got along well in spite of the fact that I had begun asking his daughter Bernice for dates when I was seventeen and she was just thirteen. Although Captain Layne and I were almost exact opposites in terms of religion and politics, I enjoyed his company and even joined the Knights of Pythias at his urging and attended meetings in his basement. The only cloud over our relationship was the fact that my own father ran an illegal card parlor. I was always afraid that one day

Captain Layne would have to arrest Edmund J. Brown, but luckily their districts never coincided.

My close workings with the police during my years as district attorney also gave me an appreciation of the problems and dangers built into their job. So when in the spring and summer of 1946 I began to hear of a gunman in Los Angeles who specialized in shooting cops, I followed the story with special interest. The first attack came in April, when two LAPD officers were wounded in a shootout as they tried to arrest a man for selling stolen electronic equipment. Two months later, California Highway Patrol officer Loren Roosevelt, a former prison guard at Folsom and once the police chief of the town of Arcadia, was killed after an exchange of gunfire with a man he had stopped to question. Roosevelt lived long enough to give detectives good information about his killer, but it was another six months before they made a spectacular arrest.

I have some of the old newspaper stories in front of me now. "Grabbing for a machine gun, one of five in his apartment, the slayer of California Highway Patrolman Loren Roosevelt was wounded and captured today," wrote the *Los Angeles Herald-Express* on December 20, 1946. "Erwin 'Machine Gun' Walker, 28, former member of the Glendale Police Department and ex-Signal Corps officer, admitted the murder of Roosevelt and the shooting of two other policemen after his capture in a gun battle. Walker's Hollywood apartment and three stolen cars found nearby offered up a cache of weapons—five machine guns and 15 other weapons, hundreds of rounds of ammunition plus homemade nitroglycerine, fake license plates and forged drivers' licenses. . . ."

The stories go on to tell how detectives, acting on a hunch that the man they wanted had inside knowledge of police methods, showed pictures of former police department employees to the victims of the April shootout and got an identification of Walker, who had been a radio dispatcher with the Glendale Police Department from 1940 to 1942 before leaving to join the Army Signal Corps. Since his return from the Pacific in 1945, Walker had been working as a radar technician and film sound man by day and an armed robber by night. Tracing him to his Hollywood hideout, three detectives broke in late at night and found Walker sleeping with a loaded machine gun on a chair next to him. He jumped out of bed and grabbed for the gun; the detectives pinned him to the floor but he wrestled free. In the struggle, Walker was shot twice, in the shoulder and chest. Doctors found the scars from two other bullet wounds which he received during the April gun battle, and which he treated himself with sulfa powder. He made a long, rambling statement in the ambulance taking him to the hospital, confessing to the Roosevelt killing and the April shootings. Learning that one of the men who caught him had a wife and two children, Walker told him, "You are very lucky—you might never have seen them again. My advice to you is that you'd better get out of this tough business if you want to enjoy your family." He also was quoted as telling the detectives, "It's too bad you guys didn't kill me. I know what I have to face and what my people have to face."

It turned out that Walker came from a solid Glendale family: his father Weston was a county engineer and one of his uncles was a superior court judge. The young man had been a very promising student of electronics at Cal Tech before the war, but after he was discharged, his family found him bitter and morose, full of guilt about the deaths of his comrades and talking wildly about a bizarre plan to end war forever by building a "death ray" that would destroy the world's weapons. Incredulous and saddened by his arrest, Walker's family nevertheless stood by him and made every effort to defend him during his trial in June 1947.

Pleading not guilty by reason of insanity, Walker waived a jury trial. Superior Court Judge Harold Landreth heard the case, and the newspaper coverage revealed more details about Walker's life during and after his military service. Trained in radar repair and maintenance, he earned the rank of second lieutenant and was made part of a Signal Corps unit which went in with advance combat troops. On Wake Island, Walker's unit was subjected to endless days and nights of Japanese bombardment. When they weren't being shelled, they had to live among the thousands of dismembered, decomposed bodies of Japanese soldiers that covered the island. On Leyte Island, Walker and another officer were put in charge of the safety of eighty-five men. Walker returned to his ship to get some equipment, and during his absence the Japanese attacked and killed more than half of the unit—including Walker's closest friend, Lieutenant Leroy Keizer, whose body Walker found beheaded in his hammock. Although an investigation cleared him of any fault, Walker claimed to feel an overwhelming sense of guilt for his failure to protect his men. Shortly after this, he requested a transfer back to the United States, where he was promoted to first lieutenant and began his life of crime.

While Walker was still on active duty, he broke into an Army warehouse at night and stole six machine guns, twelve .45 automatic pistols, six .38 revolvers, holsters, ammunition and clips, all of which he then buried near his Army base in Sacramento. Discharged in November 1945, he immediately committed a series of burglaries, stealing civilian clothes, film and sound equipment and a car on which he changed the license plates and then used to move his cache of weapons to a rented garage in the Hollywood Hills. His plan, he told Judge Landreth, was to invent an electronic radar gun that would disintegrate metal into powder, thus destroying all weapons of war. Walker also testified that he had devised this plan on the troop ship taking him home from Leyte, during a conversation with his dead friend Lieutenant Keizer about ways to prevent any future wars.

Financing his research through a series of burglaries, Walker made nitroglycerine out of stolen chemicals and used it to blow safes. While recovering from the April 1946 shootout with two policemen, he read in a book about explosives that the best way to apply nitroglycerine was with a clean chicken feather. So early on the morning of June 5, he drove to a poultry market in the Los Feliz area, cut the padlock and replaced it with one of his own, then drove around the block to see if anyone was watching.

Officer Roosevelt, on his way home, noticed a man acting suspiciously, stopped him and asked for some identification. As Walker pulled out a .45 automatic, Roosevelt reached for his own gun. Walker shot him twice and then ran away, abandoning his car, which was later found to contain a loaded Thompson submachine gun, a bag of burglar's tools, nitroglycerine, a blasting fuse and percussion caps. Roosevelt lived for several hours while fellow officers donated blood, and he provided them with a detailed description of the man who shot him, a description that finally led to Walker's arrest.

Although he denied certain parts of the confession he had supposedly made to arresting officers in the ambulance, Walker never tried to evade the responsibility for shooting Roosevelt or the two other policemen. Instead, his lawyers argued that insanity brought on by his wartime experiences was responsible for his actions. They pointed to a long history of mental problems in the family, several members of which had committed suicide or been institutionalized. Walker's parents and sister spoke sadly about the changes they saw in him on his return from the war: the once-gentle and sensitive young man had become secretive, angry, brooding, rough with small children and impossible to live with.

But the three court-appointed psychiatrists who examined Walker—all experts in criminal behavior—were unanimous in their conclusions that although he was emotionally unstable, he was legally sane both at the time of his commission of the murder of Officer Roosevelt and at the time of their examinations nine months later. One of them, Dr. R. O. Lieuallen, a staff psychiatrist at Norwalk State Hospital, testified that Walker's story about meeting the dead Lieutenant Keizer on board ship did not "ring of the true delusion or hallucination," and went on at length to explain why.

Judge Landreth listened to the evidence in the week-long trial and came back two days later with a verdict of guilty of murder in the first degree. He dismissed the insanity plea, pointing out that millions of young men had gone through equally terrible wartime experiences and were now leading normal lives. Judge Landreth said he had "searched his soul very prayerfully" and reached the conclusion that Erwin Walker, despite his obvious intelligence, would be "a menace to society wherever he is, inside or outside the penitentiary. His remarks have indicated that if he were sentenced to prison he would immediately set about finding ways of getting out, and I think the chances are fairly good that he might be successful. Because of this, I fix the penalty in this case as the death penalty provided by law."

The Walker case sounds like perfect material for a Hollywood B movie, and the 1948 film *He Walked by Night*, starring Richard Basehart as a war hero turned criminal, was indeed a fictionalized account of his story. But the Walker family never got any money from the unauthorized motion picture, and they spent what savings they had on several unsuccessful appeals. Erwin's execution date was set for June 1948. On December 11, 1947, a few hours after visiting his son on San Quentin's Death Row, fifty-eight-year-old Weston Walker committed suicide by inhaling carbon monoxide in his car, parked near the County Flood Control Basin where he had worked for twenty years. "He was spending every dime he had to save his boy from the gas chamber," a fellow worker said. "He had been despondent about it for months."

Despite the tragedy of the father's suicide, the guilty verdict and death sentence for Erwin Walker seemed to me to be a satisfactory ending to the story of a man who had killed a policeman. All the cops I knew agreed with me. Walker filed another appeal, saying the court should have reduced the charge against him to second-degree murder because of his mental condition, but the California Supreme Court denied that request and a new execution date of April 15, 1949, was set.

Prison psychiatrists continued to examine Walker: their report of February 24, 1949, found him "apparently actively hallucinating today. He has had visual hallucinations within the last ten days. He is grandiose, expansive, delusional, reclusive, bizarre and has a paranoid schizophrenic mental disorder, but knows the crime he committed and for which he has been sentenced to execution. He is aware of his present predicament." A month later, the psychiatrists wrote that he was "sad and depressed. . . . He still feels he wasn't in his right mind when his crime was committed, and for the whole time since his return from the war. . . . He is distant, detached, withdrawn, and is delusional and preoccupied. He has had no further hallucinations, but dates such phenomena to the dropping of the atomic bomb. . . ."

On April 2, Walker's lawyer made a request to Governor Earl Warren for clemency. I have a copy of Governor Warren's handwritten reply: "I have reviewed this record carefully. . . . He was found by alienists at the trial to be sane and above average in intelligence. Prison alienists found him to be sane. His only defense is insanity. The courts have found against him. I cannot find in his favor. There is nothing in the case therefore to commend him for executive clemency and it will not be granted. His only recourse is to the courts."

The next important document in the Erwin Walker file is a report dated April 14, 1949—the day before his scheduled execution—from San Quentin correctional officer F. W. McNeil to his supervisor: "At approximately 8:20 A.M. this date, while assigned to duty in the North Block Isolation Unit, I was engaged in supervising the breakfast meal. As I approached Cell 2440, I saw that the condemned inmate Walker was lying face-downward on the bed, completely covered with a blanket. . . . I called to him several times, asking him if he wanted breakfast. He made no response to my inquiry and as I could not arouse him, I opened the cell door and being mindful of a possible ruse on the part of the inmate, waited to see what took place. He still made no move to arise, whereupon I then cautiously inched toward him to pull the blanket away from him. I saw that his head was encased in a paper sack, and also that a cord or wire (later identified as the cord to his radio headset) was tightly wrapped around his neck and tied in a knot.

"I immediately set about loosening the wire, and although he said nothing, he did move, and I was aware that he was alive. I then stepped out of the cell, locked the door, and called Sergeant M. J. Todd. I quietly informed him of what had happened. He then called the hospital for a doctor and then notified the captain's office of what had taken place. Shortly thereafter, at approximately 8:30 A.M., Dr. T. L. Grayson arrived. With him, I entered the cell and removed the wire from around Walker's neck. Dr. Grayson examined Walker and stated that he apparently suffered no serious effects from the attempted suicide and that he was in good physical condition. . . ."

Walker was taken to the holding cell near the gas chamber while the people in charge decided what to do with him. California law says that no insane person can be executed, but attempting suicide isn't necessarily a sign of insanity. There was the famous case of Robert Pierce, who slashed his neck with a piece of broken glass just minutes before his execution in 1956, but the execution proceeded as scheduled, delayed for just a few minutes because the prisoner was so slippery with blood that it took five guards to finally strap him into his chair. San Quentin Warden Clinton Duffy was obviously very troubled about Walker; in the files at the California State Archives is a memo from Governor Warren's clemency secretary, James Welsh, dated April 15, 1949: "Warden Duffy called this morning at 9:00 A.M. He stated he had talked to corrections director McGee last evening. Walker is still in a completely depressed state and the Warden has called in Dr. Miller, Dr. Williams of Mendocino, Dr. Simon of Langley Porter, who with Dr. Schmidt, Dr. Rodgers and the staff at San Quentin are going over him now. The Warden stated he felt he just had to have some advice. He said Walker is completely out, you might say. The Warden didn't think it would be right without advice to take Walker in the gas chamber. The Warden states this is the first one of this extreme mental state like this. They are usually a little nervous or excited."

That same day, the special medical board convened by Warden Duffy decided that Walker was now legally insane. "We find the inmate to be negativistic, mute, fearful and unresponsive, possibly reacting to hallucinations," they wrote. "He displays a startled reaction to touch or approach. He is exhibiting definite signs and symptoms of insanity, and in our opinion at this time does not know the difference between right and wrong." At the doctors' request, Warden Duffy indefinitely postponed Walker's execution and asked the Superior Court to schedule a hearing on his sanity. That hearing was held in Marin County on May 5, 1949: a jury quickly found Walker insane and he was committed to Mendocino State Hospital. My reaction, and the reaction of the police officers I knew and worked with, was mostly angry frustration: another killer, this time a cop killer, had managed to beat the system. We stewed about it for a while, then shrugged our shoulders and went back to work.

For the next twelve years, Walker bounced around the California state mental hospital system, from Mendocino to Atascadero to Vacaville; he was a model patient and attracted little attention. By the time I became governor in 1959, I had quite frankly forgotten about his case in the crush of other criminal business up to and including Caryl Chessman. Even when Walker—who by then had been assigned to a minimum-security ward—walked away from Atascadero for three days in November 1959, the matter wasn't called to my attention. He was found by a quail hunter hiding in some bushes not far away and gave up without a struggle. Psychiatrists later blamed the episode on all the newspaper and radio stories about Chessman's imminent death in the gas chamber, which frightened Walker about his own predicament. "When he is threatened with loss of life, he becomes psychotic easily," their report said succinctly.

Erwin Walker dramatically reentered my life in December 1960, when he requested a new sanity hearing and listed me as the reason. "I would rather risk the gas chamber again by taking a chance on the clemency of Governor Brown than spend the rest of my life in a mental hospital," he said. Under Section 3704 of the California Penal Code, once a prisoner formerly sentenced to death has had that sentence set aside for reasons of insanity, a new execution date can only be set by the governor, who must "issue to the Warden his warrant appointing a day for the execution of the judgment." I didn't even have the State Supreme Court to worry about or lean on this time, because Walker had no previous felony convictions. Chessman had been dead for just seven months; the echoes and aftershocks from the public booings still filled my dreams. How could I possibly get involved in a potential political disaster like this so soon again?

If I'd known about Joseph Heller's *Catch-22* at this point, I might have wished out loud that the psychiatric panel and the judge hearing Walker's plea would decide that anyone who risks death by asking for a sanity hearing *must* be insane. Of course, they did no such thing. In February 1961, the panel said that Walker was sane "in so far as he understands the proceedings and their implications," and in March my old Chessman adversary, Judge Keating of the Marin County Superior Court, certified to me that Erwin Walker had indeed recovered his sanity. The ball was now in my court, but it looked more like a time bomb.

That year, there were three bills before the state legislature to abolish or modify capital punishment. I had promised my staff that I'd stay out of the fight, so that other bills we were starting or supporting wouldn't get caught in the crossfire, and now the Walker case threatened this fragile détente. As soon as I announced the date of his clemency hearing—March 28, 1961—calls and letters began to pour in from law enforcement people, urging me to do my job and execute him. One of the three detectives who arrested Walker said that the gunman had told other inmates at Atascadero that he would kill him if he ever got out, and that in the ambulance taking him to the hospital Walker had told him, "The only thing that I'm sorry about is that I didn't wipe you guys out." Other police officers begged me not to follow up my indecision on the Chessman case with another act of weakness, thereby sending a message to the world that California had become a safe haven for criminals.

But not all the letters I received were against clemency. Walker's mother, still working hard to defend him, gave a long story to the *Glendale News-Press* before the clemency hearing, circulated it widely and made sure that I got a copy. "When our troops re-took Leyte, in the Philippines, Erwin's captain and many members of his company were butchered by the Japanese in a sneak night attack," she wrote. "This made Erwin so crazy that all alone, he went into the Jap-infested jungle with a sub-machine gun to avenge the deaths of his comrades. There he remained a whole week. His remaining comrades, who saw him after he returned, say he expressed all the symptoms of insanity. . . . More than 20 of his remaining comrades on Leyte would have testified at Erwin's trial, to prove that after he returned from the jungle he expressed every symptom of insanity. But at the time of Erwin's trial, we just didn't have the money to employ a psychiatrist to establish his insanity, nor did we have the money to bring in the living members of his company, as most of them lived in the East. . . .

"Now, after being an insane ward of the State of California for more than 11 years, Erwin has regained his sanity," Mrs. Walker wrote. "I have talked with him and he is now the same gentle person who entered the war. His memory of all that has happened during the past 15 years is not clear. He deeply regrets the grief and harm he has caused anyone. But even though his very life is now at stake he feels that he should bravely face any penalty the authorities say he should pay. . . ."

Another pro-Walker letter came from a man who had worked with him before the war and who continued to visit him during his mental hospital years. "I have never known a more refined, well educated and sweet tempered fellow man than Erwin Walker," he wrote. "There is no question in my mind that it was his experience in combat that did something to his mind. I too was in combat in Europe, and I know that I am not the same man mentally that I was before. No doubt combat affects some more than others, and unfortunately Erwin was one of those so grossly affected. . . ."

Meanwhile, my clemency secretary Cecil Poole and investigators from the Adult Authority were putting together the "Black

Book" on the Walker case, the clemency report which hit my desk on March 27, the day before the hearing. Included in it were interviews with most of the concerned principles. Los Angeles Chief of Police William H. Parker told the investigators that in his firm opinion the people of the state of California "have provided the supreme penalty for persons committing certain crimes and, if this law is to be abolished or modified, it should be done by the legislature—not the governor. Granting clemency in this case would be an abuse of the governor's privilege, and would result in considerable censure from law enforcement agencies." Chief Parker said it was his belief that the issue of Walker's insanity was not material: his crimes were carefully planned and carried out. Captain Jack Donohoe, one of the officers who arrested Walker, was even more vehement, saying that it was a "discredit to the judicial system that he has remained alive these many years." He called attention to the fact that the two police officers shot by Walker still hadn't fully recovered from those wounds, and that Loren Roosevelt's widow and children were still suffering because of his death. Captain Donohoe also cast strong doubts on Walker's insanity, calling him "a superb actor motivated by the desire to stay alive."

Two sections of the report were of particular interest to me. The first was an interview with Walker himself, which revealed many more details of his life during and after the war. "I made a big mistake becoming an officer," he told the investigator. As a child, he explained, he had never been a joiner: he tended to avoid personal relationships and carried this attitude into the service. He was extremely anxious that the enlisted men under him would not obey his orders, and that he wouldn't know how to discipline them when that happened.

Walker described, with some hesitancy, several incidents that he thought illustrated his inadequacy as an officer. While he was on Wake Island, rumors began to circulate that the Japanese planned to recapture it. Walker said he became so concerned that he discussed with five enlisted men a plan for deserting in case of an attack—by fastening planks to gasoline drums and floating to another island on a makeshift raft. The enlisted men didn't respond with any enthusiasm, and when the attack rumors subsided Walker felt ashamed of what he saw as his cowardice.

Another time, on board a landing ship approaching an island in the Philippines, Walker suddenly threw his submachine gun into the ocean. "It was a compulsive thing," he told the investigator. "I was this little mousy person who held himself together most of the time, but who fell apart in moments of stress." He said that no one saw him throw away his weapon, and that he was able to replace it with no difficulty.

After he was discharged from the Army, Walker took his cache of stolen guns and buried them for a while under his family home in Glendale. He recalled with obvious discomfort how he put some of his discharge money down on a lot in the Hollywood Hills, where he planned to build an underground laboratory and work on his weapon designed to end war. When this proved to be too expensive, he rented a four-car garage instead and began his series of burglaries. He pointed out that his crimes were committed over a period of more than a year, and that at times in between "I would get hold of myself" and take a job. He believed he was rational at these times, and mentioned a woman to whom he was engaged and who knew nothing about his crimes.

Walker told the investigator that he attempted suicide on Death Row to help his family avoid the stigma that would come from his execution, and also to escape from what he called the "circus-like atmosphere" of a public execution. He said that he hoped his case would soon be brought to its ultimate conclusion, because the threat of death hanging over his head "paralyzes any constructive planning" about learning a trade. Asked if he had any message for me, he said, "I pray that you will grant me a commutation of sentence. You will never have cause to regret this as I know and feel inside myself that I have been completely rehabilitated. I am sorry more than words can say about all the wrongs I have committed. The only way I can make amends is to make sure I never again do anything wrong. If ever the opportunity arises where I can make amends, I shall certainly do so."

The other part of the report to which I paid particular attention was a letter from Dr. David G. Schmidt, the chief psychiatrist at San Quentin, a shrewd and compassionate man whose counsel had been valuable in the past. He spoke of Walker's family history: four suicides; a grandfather, two aunts and a cousin who spent time in mental hospitals; and several other relatives with psychiatric problems. "He was drafted into the service despite this history of instability," wrote Dr. Schmidt, "and he ended up as a war casualty, as a beautiful example of what war may do to an individual." After the attack on his company in Leyte that killed his friend Keizer, Walker himself "has no recall of exactly what followed, but his fellow servicemen have testified and are on record that he grabbed a machine gun, rushed into the jungle forest after the retreating Japs, yelling at the top of his lungs. Three or four days later, he returned to his company—disheveled, unshaved and unkempt, depressed and mute, and would not talk to people in his company, would not eat, and acted so bizarrely and disturbed that shortly thereafter he was returned to the States. When he left, he rode off in his jeep without saying a word of goodbye to any members of his company. . . ."

Dr. Schmidt described Walker's treatment at Mendocino: "He was given electroshock treatment, together with individual and group psychotherapy, and he made a slow recovery. He was seen by the writer and Warden Duffy several years later, on one of our trips to Mendocino State Hospital, and he was not then sufficiently recovered to return to the Department of Corrections. Walker was later transferred to Atascadero, where he received more individual and group psychotherapy. Among other things, he learned to play a musical instrument and he played in the band which visited surrounding communities. . . ."

It was the final paragraph of Dr. Schmidt's letter that almost leaped off the page: "Subject has been built up and his mental illness has been largely cured. His mental health has been largely restored and his schizophrenic split has been largely mended. His return to Condemned Row might again result in a mental illness, and it almost seems as though our society has

THE SOLDIER

healed the broken wing of the sparrow so that it can again fly, and that our society is now, by analogy, ready to wring the sparrow's neck. . . ."

I turned to Cecil Poole's recommendation. As always, the writing and thinking were clear and unemotional, focusing only on the issues at hand: "I do not believe that Walker's mental illness could in any degree have exonerated him from full criminal responsibility for the murder of which he was convicted. Were the Governor asked to extend executive clemency in such a case without the intervening twelve-year period, this would not seem to me a proper case for such action," Poole wrote. "The important thing in this case is that, whatever may have been the prior condition, Walker suffered a psychotic mental breakdown in 1949 and the State has spent thousands of dollars and twelve long years attempting to patch him up. Therefore, a completely different situation is presented than would have been the case had this long episode not occurred. . . .

"I believe this man should be commuted to life imprisonment. He can still be extremely dangerous, and based on that point of view as well as the enormity of his criminal past I cannot now consider the propriety of subjecting him to normal parole procedures. I therefore recommend that he be commuted without possibility of parole."

I closed the clemency report and put it away in my desk for the following morning. I had a pretty good idea of what I was going to do, but it wasn't something I wanted to talk about at home with the daughter of a police captain less than a year after the Chessman case.

It wasn't a long or crowded hearing, as those things went: gathered in my office on March 28, 1961, were Walker's lawyer, John C. Houlihan; Cecil Poole and Dr. David Schmidt; Clinton Duffy of the Adult Authority, who was warden of San Quentin when Walker attempted suicide in 1949; Department of Corrections Director Richard McGee; and Manley Bowler, chief assistant district attorney of Los Angeles, who had helped to prosecute

67

Walker in 1947. Poole opened the proceedings with a recap of the Walker family's history of insanity, then segued into a detailed recital of his life before and during World War II. Houlihan pleaded for commutation for what he described as "two compelling reasons—the good life this man led before he went into the service, and his present mental condition." Duffy, who told us that Walker's mental state was "the worst of all the hundred fifty men I've seen headed for execution," said that he had spoken with Walker for two hours yesterday at Vacaville, and while his condition has improved greatly, "I'm personally certain he will snap again if he is returned to Death Row."

I posed a question to Dr. Schmidt: "If Walker were eligible for parole today, would you parole him?" "No," he answered. "He would require a great deal more treatment." Duffy concurred, saying that it would be years before the Adult Authority would even consider the possibility of parole.

Bowler was the only person who opposed commutation. He cited the fairness of Walker's original trial and the suffering of the police officers and their families. "These are not easy things to forget," he said. "Do you think we should execute Walker?" I asked him. "Yes." he replied. "Do you really?" I pressed. "Under the laws of the state, I believe we should," Bowler said.

My decision came with what one reporter called "startling swiftness" after an hour of testimony. "I think I've heard enough about this case," I said. "I've never before commuted the sentence of a man who killed a police officer, and I hope I never have to again. There's no question that Walker was guilty, and that he got a fair trial as far as it went. But I'm also convinced that no earthly good would be served by executing him in his present state. The only question in my mind is whether I should commute the sentence with or without the possibility of parole." Poole repeated his strong arguments against parole at this time, and I agreed to leave that for future review, perhaps as early as next year.

Reaction to my decision was as swift as it was predictable. "If Machine Gun Walker is again freed to roam around among people, the probability is that he will go on another crime spree—and kill again," said an editorial the next day in the Hearst news-papers in San Francisco and Los Angeles. "How many innocent people will suffer death this time? Walker has cost the state $1000 a month for the last 14 years. . . . Must the cost be allowed to become even greater, in human lives?" Letters attached to clippings of this editorial flooded my office. The two top police officers in Los Angeles, Chief Parker and Sheriff Peter Pitchess, held a press conference to denounce my decision, saying that "law-enforcement officers and the people they protect have suf-fered a major defeat."

Maybe I was feeling guilty for having gone too far by talking openly about parole for Walker so soon. Maybe the injustice of the charge of being insensitive to the safety of the police pushed me over the edge. Maybe the strain of the Chessman case had finally gotten to me. Whatever the reason, I lashed out at Parker and Pitchess, telling reporters that "if the Sheriff and the Chief of Police were doing their jobs as well as I'm doing mine, perhaps Los Angeles wouldn't have the highest crime rate in the coun-try!" This didn't win me any new fans in the LAPD, but later Sheriff Pitchess and I became good friends and he agreed that my decision on Walker had been correct.

For the others, the thousands who wrote to express their moral outrage about my letting Walker live, I finally drafted a form letter which summed up my feelings: "Many people have written to me concerning this case. A great majority apparently approved of the action." (This was technically true if you counted the ones who called or spoke to me in person, but the letters were about evenly split.) "Some, like yourself, disapproved, feeling that Walker's execution was somehow necessary either for the morale of peace officers or for the protection of the public. Homicide, whether by crime or by the state, ought to concern all of us greatly. I do not see how we can encourage the craving for execution any more than we can approve of the original lawless killing. Emotions run high on these controversial matters, but I do not believe we are really protecting ourselves by maintaining the gas chamber.

"I have had more experience in law enforcement than most of

my critics. Walker is the only person I have ever spared who killed a peace officer. I took this action based upon the overwhelming and completely undisputed record of insanity which overcame him in 1949—long before I was Governor—and the background of 90 years of insanity in his direct ancestry. Also, without dispute, the psychiatrists told me that while Walker can now tell right from wrong and hence is legally sane, he is still medically insane and needs a great deal of additional psychiatric treatment.

"I am prepared to stand behind the principle that the State of California did not spend thousands of dollars and thousands of man hours in putting together an admittedly broken mind only for the purpose now of placing that body in the gas chamber. Surely vengeance does not live so long. I respect your right to disagree and I hope you will at least appreciate the honesty of my own decision."

Unlike the Chessman case, the uproar over Walker lasted only a few months. By summer, the letters had stopped coming in and the police were talking to me again. One day in May, I was in the Vacaville area on other business and decided to pay a surprise visit to Walker. I waited in the office as they brought in a thin, nervous, good-looking man in his forties who stood there at attention. I looked at him and a mixture of pride and amazement came over me. I said to myself, "This man would be dead if it weren't for you! There isn't another governor in the world crazy enough to commute the sentence of a convicted cop killer." Some of what I felt must have been obvious, because Walker looked at me and said, "Governor, you'll never regret it."

When I tell people the story of Machine Gun Walker and ask them how they think it ends, nine out of ten say, "He gets out of prison, grabs a machine gun and kills somebody—probably a cop." But the real ending, as much as I know about it and can reveal here, is even more dramatic. Erwin Walker responded increasingly well to psychotherapy and went to work doing medical research at San Quentin. Before I left office at the end of

1966, I did commute his sentence again, to straight life. A leading San Francisco psychiatrist took an interest in his case, as did a lawyer from one of that city's major law firms. Together, they helped Walker get out of prison, in 1974, under RUAPP (Released Under Approved Parole Plan). Then, in 1978, Walker received a full discharge from parole under a new California law. That same year, he used his undoubted brilliance and electronic skill to design a remarkable piece of computer technology that earned him a sizable amount of money. With that money, he decided to change his name and move to a new location, leaving his past far behind him. I haven't heard a word about him in ten years, but I wish him well.

CHAPTER FOUR

Damaged Brains

So far, I've talked about the political side of executive clemency in the abstract: what impact my decisions might have on my reputation, or on a spectrum of bills we were trying to enact. In the case of Richard Lindsey, the political issue became much more specific: if I spared this man's life, I would almost certainly be dooming an important farm labor minimum-wage bill that we had worked hard to promote.

The details of the Lindsey case are so horrible that even now, twenty-seven years later, I shudder when I think about them. It is the kind of crime that stirs up public emotion and stretches the most liberal anti–death-penalty convictions to their breaking point. But I have to tell you what happened so that you can begin to understand the atmosphere in which my decision was made.

Richard Arlen Lindsey was thirty, an alcoholic drifter from Texas with a history of violence against his family that had caused him to be arrested and confined for short periods at various mental facilities. Dishonorably discharged from the Army at the age of eighteen, after just nine months of service, he spent half of the next twelve years in prisons in Texas, Arkansas and Oklahoma for car theft, grand larceny and taking a woman across state lines for sexual purposes. He had been married six times, the first time when he was sixteen, each marriage ending in some episode of actual or threatened violence. In 1960, he met the woman who had been his third wife, Dixie Elaine Lindsey, in a bar in Texas and began living with her again. On January 12, 1961, with the twenty-three-year-old Dixie seven months pregnant and the couple staying at a farm labor camp near Bakersfield, California, Richard told his wife that he wanted to have sex with a little girl.

The pair drove to another farm labor camp near the town of Shafter, where Dixie Lindsey talked to several children and offered them a dollar to help clean her house. She finally induced six-year-old Rose Marie Riddle to get into the car. After a stop for food and brake fluid in the town of Wasco, they drove to the isolated Lost Hills area of Kern County, near Blackwell, where they parked the car in a heavy fog and the Lindseys drank some whiskey. According to Dixie Lindsey's subsequent statement, when the little girl began to cry and demanded to be taken home, she slapped her and said to her husband, "We might as well get it over with."

Dixie Lindsey got into the rear seat of the car while her husband brutally raped the little girl, causing severe damage to her internal organs. Richard Lindsey then choked the Riddle child until she appeared to be dead, took the body and left it about forty yards away in some brush. As the couple started to leave, they heard noises from the area. "Well, you didn't kill her but I will," said Dixie Lindsey. She took a heavy tire wrench from the car and beat the child about the head at least sixteen times. Then she and her husband drove away. Physical evidence later showed that the Riddle girl crawled about fifteen feet after the beating before she died.

The Lindseys drove toward San Francisco, where they checked into a motel, but their black, four-door 1950 Chevrolet with Texas license plates made them an easy target. When Rose Marie Riddle was first declared missing and details of the Lindseys and their car were sent out on January 14, police officers in the town of Tracy remembered stopping them for faulty brakes the day before near the Oakland Bay Bridge. Later on the fourteenth, the police spotted the Lindsey car pulled off the side of the road between Tracy and Oakland. Richard and Dixie, who had stopped to have a nap, were arrested for kidnapping. Three days later, when the Riddle girl's body was found, rape and murder were added to the charges.

Both Lindseys were arraigned in Bakersfield on January 17, and because they had no money the court appointed a separate attorney for each of them. Preliminary hearings were set for February 1, but on January 20, Richard Lindsey and his court-appointed lawyer asked to waive the preliminary hearing, entered a plea of guilty on all counts, and decided also to give up his right to have a full jury decide on his penalty. "Is it your desire to waive the jury on the matter of penalty and throw yourself on the mercy of the Court?" his lawyer asked. "Yes, sir," Lindsey replied. Ten days later, after hearing testimony from three psychiatrists and from Lindsey's mother, Judge William L. Bradshaw sentenced Richard Lindsey to death. (Because of her pregnancy, Dixie Lindsey's trial was postponed; she was later sentenced to life in prison without possibility of parole.)

By the time of his automatic appeal to the California Supreme Court in June, Richard Lindsey had a new lawyer, obtained by his parents, who contended that the court-appointed attorney had been grossly negligent and that doubts about Lindsey's sanity should have been raised more strongly during the penalty phase. But a unanimous opinion by the Supreme Court on July 24 upheld Judge Bradshaw's decision, and an execution date of November 14, 1961, was set. Lindsey's attorney asked for a clemency hearing, which was scheduled for November 7. Cecil Poole had left my staff in April 1961 to become the first black U.S. Attorney for Northern California, and I had appointed a young prosecutor of Hispanic descent from Los Angeles, Arthur Alarcon, to be my second clemency secretary. Alarcon's "Black Book" on the Lindsey case was completed on November 3.

* * *

One of the primary goals of my administration when we took office in 1959 was to pass a minimum-wage law for migrant farm workers, so that these hard-pressed laborers would not have to exist on whatever the growers decided to pay them from week to week. In one of the many sad ironies of the Lindsey case, this bill designed to help people like the parents of Rose Marie Riddle was finally being argued by the Agriculture Committee of the state legislature during the same week Richard Lindsey's clemency hearing was conducted. It looked like a close call: we had seven sure votes on the fifteen-member committee, but the important swing vote belonged to a legislator from Kern County, where the crime had occurred. This man was a strong advocate of the death penalty; he had publicly made known his view that Richard Lindsey should die, and had told me in private that if I commuted the sentence his district would, in his words, "go up in smoke." This was very much on my mind as I read the clemency file on Richard Arlen Lindsey.

On the issue of Lindsey's sanity, Alarcon's report covered the testimony of the psychiatrists in a few brief sentences. All three said that while Lindsey did have what they called a "sociopathic character disorder," he was in their opinion legally sane. I saw that in March 1958 Lindsey's mother had committed him to Terrell State Hospital in Texas for a ninety-day period of observation because of violent behavior toward some elderly neighbors. He was out in forty-eight days; but a few weeks later his father again had him committed after another violent outburst. The clemency report noted that Lindsey's mother had testified about his violent temper tantrums dating from early childhood. She mentioned a serious automobile accident in 1956, when Lindsey suffered a fractured skull, and said that his conduct became more violent after that.

There was also an interview with Richard Lindsey in the file, conducted by two investigators from the Adult Authority. "It did not appear that he readily understood the purpose of the interview and it was necessary to explain in detail that we were there to obtain from him any information which he felt should be available to Governor Brown when he reviewed the case," wrote the investigators. "He seldom volunteered any information and frequently seemed confused at questions directed to him."

Lindsey told the interviewers that he was certain he was guilty of the attack on Rose Marie Riddle, but at the same time "it doesn't seem like I did it." He said that he didn't recall anything from the time he started to work that morning until he found himself in a motel room in San Francisco that night. He did remember that he and Dixie had consumed quantities of wine and whiskey before the victim was accosted. "I just don't know what the deal was," he said. "I didn't have any reason to do this. Anyone who knows me will tell you I have always been good to kids. I have never done any real bad crimes."

The investigators asked Lindsey about his acts of violence toward his father, his former wives and his neighbors. He could not explain any of them, and claimed to love and respect his parents very much. His message for me was this: "I don't particularly want to die. I always try to take things as they are. If I die it won't solve that which has already happened. I ain't going to cry about it. I don't want out unless I can go to a hospital to be all right. I don't think I'm crazy but there is something wrong. I should stay in prison the rest of my life if not cured."

There was a letter to me from Judge Bradshaw in the file. "I am quite reluctant to impose the death penalty in any case," he wrote, "and yet I do feel that in certain types of crimes that seems to be the only equitable penalty which can appropriately be given. I will not go into the details of this offense as I am sure they are before you from other sources, but it was my belief and still is my belief that if ever any offense justified the death penalty it was this one. I say that both because of the heinousness of the offense and the apparent utter lack of moral sensibilities of the defendant himself. There was no evidence of any type to indicate that any rehabilitation could be effected. He was classified by the psychiatrists as anti-social but without any psychosis of any type. I feel, therefore, that only the death penalty in this case would accomplish justice."

Kern County Sheriff LeRoy F. Galyen didn't spare me any of the details of Lindsey's crime in his letter; he even included a few which I might have missed. "This crime committed by Richard Lindsey was one of the worst crimes ever committed in Kern County. And from talking to other Sheriffs in the State of California, they never heard of any so vicious," he wrote. "If you think the people of Kern County are not wrought up over this, we still have hundreds and hundreds of calls if a child is missing from school or doesn't get home within a half an hour why mothers are screaming. . . .

"We had many threatening letters and there was a group of people from Shafter, I think it was mostly the whiskey talking, who were going to come down and take Lindsey out and they were going to lynch him," Sheriff Galyen went on. "Then, too, many of them had gone through our new jail and couldn't find their way out after they were turned loose, so they decided they had better not do that—they might get in there and never get out. So they decided to kidnap the Sheriff, and his ransom would be to turn Lindsey over to them. But then the fact that they knew I was no easy one to get hold of and was pretty fast on the draw, they didn't attempt that. So, the many letters that came in said that hanging or the death penalty as it was was too good for this Lindsey; that he should die the same way that the little Riddle girl did. . . . I do hope that the sentence of the court is carried out and at the nearest time. That the particular date he is supposed to die, that is the date we should get this over with and get these people out of law enforcement's hair here in Kern County. . . ."

My clemency secretary's recommendation was straightforward: "The Governor should not intervene in this case," Alarcon wrote. "There are insufficient mitigating circumstances to justify a commutation of the sentence of death imposed in this matter. Since Lindsey has been convicted of three prior felonies, Supreme Court approval would be required if a commutation were thought to be appropriate. . . . Lindsey is an extremely dangerous sociopath with a record of violent behavior dating back to his early boyhood. . . . This case has probably caused more public concern and interest in Kern County than any other in recent history. Lindsey's present attorney claims the trial attorney was incompetent. Lindsey pleaded guilty to this crime. Had he asked for a jury trial and been defended by any other attorney he could not have escaped a death penalty on these facts."

There was one more document in the file, a letter to me from Richard Lindsey's mother. Written on lined paper in a clear, rough hand, it began, "Dear Governor Brown: Here are some things I hope you will think about when you decide what to do with my son Richard," and went on for a dozen pages. "When he was a boy and changed into a man he never did develop right," she wrote. "He would just go into mad tantrums which his father and I at first thought was meanness and punish him for it. Neighbors who saw him would say, 'You people should have a doctor with him. He's not normal.' He would go out on a trip and get mad and just lie down in front of the car in the highway and refuse to move unless something was agreed on some way. He married between 16 and 17; the girl was between 14 and 15. She came to our house one night, saying he tried to smother her with a pillow. They'd be riding in the car and he'd look at her glassy-eyed, quit talking, and backhand her and slap her when they had not even been fussing. Then he'd go on a piece and stop the car and cry, saying he didn't mean to do it, didn't know why he did it. These tantrums didn't last long, and when he didn't have them there was no human under the sun sweeter or any better than Richard. . . ."

Mrs. Lindsey went on to describe the 1956 car accident in which "his head was so badly injured it was kept packed in ice for seven weeks and five days. They didn't set his broken collar bone or fix his back, thinking all the time he would die. After he came out of that, he seemed to have his tantrums more often, and they lasted longer." In the winter of 1957, for example, she told how her son attacked his wife with a knife "suddenly, for no reason," cutting her across the forehead. At the hospital, Richard's wife told the police, "He don't need to be put in no jail. He needs to be put in some mental institution for treatment." After this episode,

Lindsey's parents took him to see a psychiatrist in Oklahoma City. "He said he would treat Richard for $30 every other day, but when we told him we didn't have that kind of money he said there was nothing he could do."

A few weeks later came the incident of the threats and abusive language to an elderly couple he'd known all his life. Mrs. Lindsey said that when a friend of Richard's told him to stop, "he stuck a knife in his arm and ran off down the road, hollering 'Whoopee, I'm a wild Indian!' He wasn't drunk, but his eyes were all glassy and big—he didn't even look like himself. . . . He walked up to the old people's house late that afternoon and told the officer guarding it that he didn't remember what he'd said but he thought it was something pretty awful and he wanted to apologize. It was after this that I took him over to Terrell State for the first time. But they didn't do anything for him, just put him on some Thorazine, and 48 days later they let him go, saying he was better."

Richard had been out of the hospital less than two months when he attacked his father for no apparent reason, knocking him down. Then, when Mrs. Lindsey screamed, "he came to like he'd been slapped, saw his father on the floor and cried, 'Daddy, what are you doing down there?' After that his father took him back to Terrell State, but this time they didn't give him any medicine or anything, just locked him up in the violent ward for 50 days and then let him go again."

Mrs. Lindsey concluded her letter with these words: "Governor Brown, I hope you can see from this that my son has been sick for a long time. We tried to get him some help but it didn't do no good, nobody wanted to listen. You are his last chance."

It was late at night when I finished reading Mrs. Lindsey's letter. I was alone in the living room of the Governor's Mansion; everyone else had gone to bed. Even though she had written as an advocate, as a mother trying desperately to save her son's life, it was obvious to me that what she said had the unmistakable ring of truth. There *was* something mentally wrong with Richard Lindsey; there had been something wrong with him for a long

time and it had gotten worse since his accident in 1956. But was
he insane under the law, crazy enough to avoid the death penalty? Several psychiatrists had testified that he was not: that
while he was definitely a sociopath—someone who exhibits anti-
social behavior—he was not a psychopath—someone who is
mentally deranged. And even if he had been officially labeled a
psychopath, Lindsey would still have had to fail another crucial
test before he could be certified as legally insane: the M'Naghten
Rule, which dealt solely with a defendant's ability to distinguish
right from wrong.

I went back to the clemency file to check one last thing: the
results of Lindsey's compulsory brain-wave test. The reason he
was given one when he first arrived on Death Row had to do with
the case of another convicted murderer, a man named Vernon
Atchley.

Atchley was a borderline mental defective with an IQ of only 60
who couldn't read or write anything but his name. But he had an
unusual talent for business, and made a good living selling used
cars, renting property and running a tavern and an eighty-acre
ranch in the Northern California community of Palermo, near
Oroville, in Butte County. He was thirty-nine and living with his
secretary-bookkeeper, a woman called Jewel Spoon, when he got
involved with Marcella Farris, who had five children by previous
liaisons. When Marcella and her children moved into Atchley's
home in 1956, Jewel Spoon first retired to a trailer behind the
house and later left town. Vernon and Marcella drank heavily and
quarreled frequently, but in 1957 they went to Georgia and got
married—a fact they kept quiet so as not to cause a reduction in
the welfare payments she was getting from Butte County.

Marriage did nothing to temper relations between the At-
chleys, however, and in July 1958 Marcella and her children
moved to a house in the nearby town of Gridley. Although Vernon
helped with the move, a fight broke out and Marcella called the
police. Vernon then told the county welfare office that she was
married to him, and she in turn told the police that Vernon had

been selling used cars without a license. Thus, all was not well between them on the night of August 2, 1958, when, hearing rumors that Marcella had been dating other men, Vernon began drinking and then drove to Gridley to confront her. She wasn't home, so he drove around looking for her, stopping at several taverns en route, and finally came back to her house about midnight. He took from his glove compartment a .22 pistol loaded with six bullets, tucked it into the waistband of his trousers and hid in Marcella's backyard where he could see the lights of her car when it arrived.

When Marcella finally came home at about 2:30 A.M., after attending a dance at the neighboring hamlet of Robinson's Corners, Atchley was waiting in her carport. Neighbors heard her scream "Oh, don't, don't!" followed by six shots. While Vernon ran for his car and drove back to Palermo, where he buried the gun in his backyard and went to bed, Marcella's neighbors and her children found her dead from six bullets, including one in the back.

Vernon Atchley, pleading self-defense because, he said, his wife had grabbed for the gun when he tried to merely frighten her with it, was brought to trial in the very same Butte County Superior Court where one of his brothers had already been convicted of murder three years before, and where the wife of a third brother had also within recent memory been released after killing her husband in self-defense. Atchley was found guilty of first-degree murder with the special circumstance of lying-in-wait, which made him eligible for the death penalty. His sentence was confirmed by the California Supreme Court, and he was originally scheduled to die in the gas chamber on March 25, 1960. I granted him a sixty-day reprieve at that point, because the state legislature was about to vote on my proposed moratorium on the death penalty, but when that failed, his execution was set for August 23, 1961. He thereby became one of Arthur Alarcon's first cases as my clemency secretary.

Arthur and I had agreed from the start that the most important part of his job was to make sure that the death penalty was administered equally in all fifty-eight California counties. "What I plan to do is look at each case from the perspective of a Los Angeles district attorney in a busy office and ask myself, 'Would this case merit a first-degree murder charge and a death penalty in L.A. County?' " he told me. After studying the Atchley file for a few days, he used that yardstick and recommended that I commute his sentence to life without possibility of parole. I asked him why. "The first thing that strikes me is that in L.A. County a husband-and-wife dispute is *never* a death-penalty case," he said. "It's classified as a crime of passion, usually a second-degree murder charge. If I'd been prosecuting and he pleaded guilty, I probably would have agreed to voluntary manslaughter and it would never have gotten to a jury. Then there's the record of Atchley's two brothers. They were a violent, hard-drinking family, outcasts in a small community, which probably produced a tainted jury pool."

I thought for a moment. "That's not good enough," I told Alarcon. "You're going to have to do a better job of convincing me."

Arthur looked surprised, as well he might: I was the one who was supposed to be against capital punishment while he supported it, and here our roles were reversed. But he returned to the Atchley file and was soon back in my office with something more solid.

In the file was a note from a San Quentin psychiatrist, who said that Atchley had told him about taking "a lick in the head" during a baseball game in 1956 that left him unconscious for a full day. Since that time, the note said, Atchley suffered from recurring nightmares and insomnia. Doctors who examined him said they had found no evidence of brain damage, but searching through the file Alarcon discovered that Atchley had never been given an electroencephalograph (EEG) test to measure his brain waves. "I'd like you to authorize an EEG for him right now," said Arthur, and I agreed. The test—administered by John Crooker, the very first man whose death sentence I commuted—showed evidence of serious brain damage in the area that controls emotional stability. Given this evidence, Vernon Atchley's case clearly fell under the Durham Rule of the federal courts, which states that if a criminal act is the product of mental deficiency or disease it is not punishable. I had no choice but to commute his sentence to life without possibility of parole. The district attorney of Butte County agreed; "If I had known about the brain damage, I would never have asked for the death penalty," he told me later.

When Warden Fred Dickson of San Quentin went to tell Atchley about the commutation, just thirty-six hours before his scheduled execution, he found Vernon playing cards with some other condemned men. "I have some good news for you," the warden said. "The governor has commuted your sentence." Atchley looked up from his cards for a moment. "Well, what do you know?" he said mildly. "Whose deal is it?"

Because of the Atchley case, I had ordered that all prisoners sent to Death Row be given an EEG test as a matter of routine. But there was no help for Richard Lindsey—or me—in that area: according to the clemency file, "his brain wave studies show an abnormal pattern which is compatible with grand mal or petit mal epileptic *susceptibility,* but he has had no actual *convulsions.*" The Durham Rule didn't apply here.

Inside the quiet Governor's Mansion late that November night, I became in a very real sense a scale of justice. The case against Lindsey was loaded with horrible details of the savage brutality that can lie hidden inside a human being until something makes it erupt. It was the kind of crime which seemed to cry out for vengeance, for ritual punishment as swift and terrible as the act itself.

Weighed against this were the doubts raised by his mother's letter about Lindsey's mental history, an issue that I felt had never really been carefully explored during his trial. Then, too, if the death penalty was designed to be a deterrent against future crimes, I couldn't for the life of me see how killing Lindsey would keep another madman from attacking another little girl somewhere down the road.

I had been governor for almost three years, and in spite of some setbacks I had managed to get a lot done. I was fighting a conservative legislature to spend more money on a growing state, to improve its schools and its mental health facilities and its working conditions. Should I risk, did I even have the *right* to risk, destroying any of that because of one demented criminal?

Rose Marie Riddle was dead, and nothing I could do would bring her back. By letting Richard Lindsey go to the gas chamber, I was giving her parents and people like them a chance at a living wage. The scales tipped. I picked up my pen and on the first page of the clemency file wrote these words: "I will take no action." I dated it November 10, 1961, and signed my name. Four days later, Lindsey was dead. That same week, the farm labor bill passed through committee and a few months later was signed into law.

Why, then, has the Lindsey case troubled me all these years— more than Chessman, more even than Edward Simon Wein, about whom you'll read in the next chapter? It has to do with the nature of legal insanity, with protecting society from mad dogs while recognizing that men are not dogs, with forcing a governor to make psychiatric judgment calls so final that the possibility of error takes on terrifying proportions.

Just how mad do you have to be to avoid the death penalty? What kind of crazy people is society allowed to kill? Theoretically, none at all: the law is firm in saying that civilized societies must protect their weakest members. "An act committed by an insane person, though otherwise unlawful, is not criminal" is the language used by California; other jurisdictions have similar wordings. But then this same law goes on to give such a narrow definition of legal insanity that many of history's most celebrated lunatics fall outside it.

The M'Naghten Rule, for instance, holds that in order for an accused person to be declared legally insane his mental faculties must be so diseased and deranged as to render him incapable of distinguishing right from wrong in relation to the act with which he is charged. I've always had trouble with M'Naghten, especially in terms of timing. A week after the fact, when he was examined by psychiatrists, Richard Lindsey probably *was* aware that what he had done was wrong—so he was legally sane. But on the day of the crime, egged on by his wife, his brain warped by alcohol and lust, who can say what moral lines were crossed or blurred?

The M'Naghten Rule dates from nineteenth-century England, and in the last several years many states—including California—have adopted a much broader definition of legal insanity, patterned after a standard model written by the American Law Institute. The ALI Rule says that a person is legally insane, even though he knows right from wrong, if he is unable "to conform his conduct to the requirements of the law"—thus recognizing that in many kinds of mental illness the person may have little or no control over his behavior.

If the ALI Rule had been in effect while I was governor, at least six other cases of my fifty-nine would probably never have reached the clemency stage—and perhaps the mental illness of the men involved would have been better treated in a medical facility than in a prison environment. It's hard to feel sympathy for any of these men, or for Richard Lindsey or Vernon Atchley, when you think about the victims of their crimes. But it's also important to remember that every country in the world, no matter how otherwise repressive or backward, makes some provision for not killing people who are mentally damaged.

James Merkouris, for example, violently threatened his ex-wife and her new husband for *six years* before he finally shot both of them to death. At his trial, he attacked the prosecutor and had to be literally caged in a Plexiglas box before the proceedings could continue. But he was declared legally sane and given the death penalty. When I saw his highly abnormal EEG readings, I had no choice but to commute his sentence to life without possibility of parole. His prison career was marked with violent incidents, and he finally died of a brain hemorrhage after attacking another inmate.

Bertrand Joseph Howk, for another example, had obviously been a walking time bomb since the age of eight—a genetic accident waiting for a time and place to happen. Brilliant, deeply troubled and grotesquely overweight, he converted to the Moslem faith when he was eighteen and changed his name to Mohammed Abdullah. Two years later, studying Islamic history and philosophy at Berkeley, he met a young woman named Sonia Hoff who didn't seem to be put off by his odd appearance and behavior. Mistaking her friendliness for the romantic interest which he so desperately wanted, he proposed marriage and then repeatedly threatened her life when she refused him. Abdullah eventually killed Miss Hoff by firing two bullets into her head, then tried to kill himself by shooting a bullet into his right temple. He survived this crude lobotomy, but at his trial he was reduced to a shambling, giggling idiot. Despite this, despite testimony about violent acts against his mother dating back a dozen years, and despite evidence that many witnesses including a Berkeley security guard had overheard his repeated threats against Miss Hoff but had taken no action except to have him expelled from the university, Abdullah was also declared legally sane and sentenced to die. His suicide attempt made EEG evidence unreliable, but when Arthur Alarcon reported a plea from an attorney who had been present at the trial—"You have to do something; he obviously had no idea what was going on and was unfit to be tried," the man told Alarcon—I again had no choice but to commute Abdullah's sentence. His prison life wasn't as violent as Merkouris's, but three years later he finally succeeded in killing himself.

And then there was Clarence Ashley, a man whose crime frighteningly mirrored Richard Lindsey's and whose psychiatric history shows just how hard it is even for teams of experts to decide when and if a person is legally sane. Like Lindsey, Ashley raped and killed the six-year-old daughter of a family of migrant farm workers—this time near the town of Gustine, in Merced County. Unlike Lindsey, Ashley was well spoken and above average in intelligence, a seventeen-year veteran of the U.S. Army who at the age of thirty-five had risen to the rank of warrant officer attached to the legal unit. The crime took place in August

1960; Ashley was arrested soon after and confessed his guilt. Two court-appointed psychiatrists examined him and decided that he was suffering from acute schizophrenia, was unable to assist counsel in the preparation or conduct of his defense, and was legally insane. In September 1960, a superior court judge ordered Ashley to be confined at Atascadero State Hospital.

Seventeen months later, Ashley was back in court, presumably sane enough to stand trial. One doctor who had examined him at Atascadero felt he was "more or less putting on an act and is not as insane as he would like people to think"; another said he was "still psychotic" and recommended further care and treatment. An Army psychiatrist who saw him at Atascadero wrote: "Schizophrenic reaction, paranoid type, chronic, severe, in partial remission, manifested by auditory and visual hallucinations, feelings of depersonalization, ideas of reference and influence, suspiciousness, tenuous control of hostility. . . ." But the consensus of expert opinion seemed to be that Ashley had improved to the point where he could assist and cooperate with his attorney, although the official report did warn that if he was cross-examined "he would certainly tend to give irrational answers."

When Ashley's trial began in February 1962, the accused turned down the services of a public defender and insisted on representing himself—whereupon the judge asked for another psychiatric reading. A three-doctor panel found that Ashley was sane enough to understand the nature of the legal proceedings against him. As the trial proceeded, these same psychiatrists testified that in their opinion Ashley was legally sane under the M'Naghten Rule at the time of the crime, adding: "It is further the tentative opinion of the examiners that such active mental illness as was later manifested was precipitated a number of days following the time during which the acts charged were committed." What these experts were saying was that, after almost two years, they could still be relatively certain that Ashley was sane when he committed his crimes, went crazy shortly thereafter, and was now sane enough again to stand trial.

The trial lasted six days, with Ashley representing himself and testifying like a runaway train as the only defense witness, after which the jury deliberated for seventeen minutes and found him guilty. On his plea of not guilty by reason of insanity, the jury took another thirty-six minutes to find him sane, and in the penalty phase of the trial the same jury spent just over an hour deciding that Ashley deserved the death penalty. He arrived on San Quentin's Death Row in May 1962 and for the next thirteen months was subjected to a further barrage of psychiatric tests. His first EEG test seemed to indicate abnormal brain waves, but these were blamed on the electroshock therapy he received at Atascadero; a subsequent test showed normal waves. A panel of doctors at San Quentin diagnosed Ashley as a "sociopathic, emotionally unstable personality with paranoid schizophrenia with expansive grandiose and persecutory delusions, with psychosexual problems and conflicts and auditory and visual hallucinations. . . ." *But,* this same panel said, "he knows the crime that he committed and for which he has been sentenced to execution and he is, therefore, sane."

While he was on Death Row, Ashley's speech and writing became so bizarre and delusional, so filled with strange religious symbolism, that Warden Fred Dickson decided to send him to the Vacaville Medical Facility for still more psychiatric tests. "Schizophrenic reaction, paranoid type, in partial remission," was the diagnosis from the panel; an outside expert from Napa State Hospital concluded that Ashley's "defective judgement and disordered conceptualization and interpretation are products of his abnormal personality whose severity is enough, in my opinion, to diagnose him as psychotic."

All of these at least partly contradictory psychiatric reports and more were waiting for me when I opened Clarence Ashley's clemency file two weeks before his scheduled execution in June 1963. It was like some kind of bizarre multiple-choice quiz. Was he (a) legally sane at the time of his crime but over the edge now; or (b) legally sane then and faking insanity now to save his life; or (c) insane all of his life and getting worse; or (d) none of the above? Most important, how was I, a lawyer and prosecutor and elected official, supposed to make a final judgment about a man's life or death when psychiatric experts with hundreds of years of training and experience among them couldn't?

Because of the doubts raised by the medical testimony, I commuted Clarence Ashley's sentence to life without possibility of parole. In 1978, after fifteen years of trouble-free incarceration at Folsom, a change in the law allowed him to apply for and be granted parole. His record since then has been clean.

We were lucky, of course. For good reason, the specter of the psychotic criminal mistakenly freed from custody to strike again has become a part of the fuel that keeps the fires of capital punishment burning. In the last decade, the combination of funding cutbacks and a loosening of the federal and state laws have prematurely returned many mental patients to society, a large portion of them unable to cope with its demands. How can a jury or a judge send a sexual psychopath to a mental hospital and be certain he'll stay there until he's cured? One answer—now being adopted in a few states—is to replace the verdict of "not guilty by reason of insanity" with one that says "guilty but mentally ill." Under this verdict, the convicted criminal can't be released merely on the word of a psychiatric panel: there has to be a full court hearing before a jury or a panel of judges.

I hope that wider acceptance of this "guilty but mentally ill" verdict might keep some future governor from having to weigh a human life against pending legislation.

CHAPTER FIVE

The Luck of Eddie Wein

Edward Simon Wein was arrested on a fluke, pardoned in error and recaptured by coincidence. He was also the worst mistake I ever made, the kind of mistake that can undo years of hard work and good intentions.

For a period of eighteen months, from early 1955 through October 1956, women who lived in various areas of Los Angeles were subjected to the attacks of a vicious and cunning rapist. Soft-spoken and neatly dressed, usually in a jacket and tie, he would answer classified ads in neighborhood newspapers offering items for sale or rooms for rent. If the person who placed the ad was a woman and appeared to be alone in the house, he would go through the motions of examining the item offered, then distract her attention by pretending to have dropped his watch stem or his watch crystal somewhere on her floor. As the woman knelt to help him look for the missing part, he would grab her from behind, menace her with a knife, bind her hands with copper wire and force her into acts of sexual perversion.

Because of the wide area he covered, and because not all of his victims reported the attacks, the police were hampered in mounting a full-scale search for the rapist. Then, in November 1956, they got a break. A woman attending a party being held in a bar in Long Beach accidentally stepped on a man's foot. She apologized, he looked up to acknowledge it and shrug it off, and she recognized him as the man who had raped and sodomized her in her Hollywood Hills home the month before. She turned away quickly, hoping the recognition wasn't mutual, went to a phone booth nearby and called the police. When they arrived minutes later, the man was still there. He identified himself as Edward Simon Wein, "Eddie" to his friends, a thirty-three-year-old Los Angeles painting contractor who had recently separated from his wife because she was upset by his gambling losses. "That gal is drunk," he told arresting officers, denying that he had ever seen his accuser before.

Wein's denials and claims of mistaken identity never faltered as victim after victim came forward to identify him as the man who had attacked them in a similar fashion after answering an ad. Seven women and a fourteen-year-old girl eventually gave testimony against the quiet, mousy-looking Wein; another woman thought he was the man who had raped her but couldn't be absolutely sure. He was charged with three counts of robbery, six counts of rape, six counts of sex perversion, and—because he had moved his victims from room to room during some of the crimes—two counts of kidnapping and five counts of kidnapping for the purpose of robbery. This last, under Penal Code Section 209, known as the "Little Lindbergh Law," called for the death penalty if bodily harm was involved. Wein also closely matched the description of a man seen outside the home of a young San Fernando Valley housewife who had been raped and stabbed to death in January 1956, but no other evidence was ever discovered to link him to this crime.

The trial of the man the newspapers called the "Want Ad Rapist" got under way in April 1957. Wein was prosecuted by J. Miller Leavy, the deputy district attorney who had asked for and received the death penalty for Caryl Chessman on similar charges some years before. Chessman was back in the news because of a recent successful appeal for a new trial, and Leavy made sure the jury didn't miss the connection. "Why, this fellow puts Caryl Chessman to shame!" he said. "He makes Chessman look like a rank amateur, a schoolboy!" Later, talking about Wein's youngest victim, Leavy said, "Chessman, too, had ice water in his veins. That little girl will carry a mark on her forever. She may end up the same way Mary Alice Meza, the seventeen-year-old virgin, the victim of the Chessman attack, did, in a mental institution, unless she has a strong mind and can in some way through her religious thinking beat it."

As Leavy played the jury like a grand piano, addressing them individually by name and whipping up their feelings of patriotism and morality, Wein's eight accusers took the stand to recount stories of fear and degradation that differed only in small, interior details. A fourteen-year-old schoolgirl wept as she told about being attacked in the basement of her family's home after letting a man she identified as Wein in to look at some furniture they had for sale. "He threatened to kill me and my little brothers and sister if I made any noise," she said. "I was so scared that I didn't know what to do." A twenty-two-year-old Hollywood model said that Wein, responding to a classified ad for a room for rent, forced her at knifepoint to remove all her clothing and perform an act of oral sex, then ordered her into a nearby bedroom where he raped her. A thirty-seven-year-old San Fernando Valley woman who advertised a mattress for sale pointed out Wein as the man who threatened her and her six-year-old son with a knife if she didn't submit to a sexual attack. Other victims ranging in age from their mid-forties to fifty-seven told similar stories, all but one involving the ruse of a dropped watch stem or crystal to put them off their guard and into a vulnerable position.

Although Wein continued to proclaim his innocence and managed to come up with credible alibis for the times of two of the attacks, the expensive celebrity lawyer paid for by his family was no match for Leavy. When Wein testified that he had never answered a want ad in his life, the prosecution produced a woman who identified him as the man who had bought a stove from her some months before and had paid for it with a worthless check—which she kept. A handwriting expert testified that the "Robert Butler" signature on the check matched Wein's writing. Two teenagers who remembered seeing a strange car parked outside one victim's house on the day of her attack underwent hypnosis and came up with a further description and part of a license number—which matched a car loaned to Wein that day by a friend. And a fingerprint expert testified that a partial print taken from a water glass at the apartment of the twenty-two-year-old victim definitely belonged to the accused man.

Wein's first plea was "not guilty by reason of insanity," but in the early days of jury selection he changed that to simply "not guilty." Aside from his alibis for the times of two of the crimes—which prosecutor Leavy managed to bury under a mountain of scorn—Wein's defense consisted mainly of witnesses who testified as to his exemplary work habits, first in his family's paint business and then on his own; his Army record, including a good-conduct medal and an honorable discharge; his strong family background, first as a son and brother and then as a man who legally adopted his wife's daughter by a previous marriage and did volunteer work at her school. Wein himself insisted to reporters that the whole affair was a tragic case of mistaken identity. "I didn't do these things," he said. "I wouldn't do these things and I couldn't do these things."

Eddie Wein's trial lasted three weeks, and it took the jury of seven women and five men just eight hours to agree that he was guilty on all counts. Since they pointedly made no recommendation for life imprisonment on the "Little Lindbergh" counts, Judge Leroy Dawson said that he had no choice but to sentence Wein to death. "Mark my words," the condemned man told reporters. "If I go to the gas chamber, those women who identified me in court will be haunted to their graves."

His execution was scheduled for September 1957, but a judge granted him a stay so that the U.S. Supreme Court could hear a plea for a new trial. It was denied; another execution date was set; another stay was granted for another appeal. Then, after further rejections by both the U.S. and California supreme courts and two denials of requests for clemency by Governor Goodwin Knight, Eddie Wein became my personal problem: he was due to die on June 5, 1959. The Chessman case was boiling away as Wein's clemency file landed on my desk.

My first thought was, "My God, just what I need—another 'Little Lindbergh' mess!" As I've already noted, I always had serious doubts about kidnapping as a death-penalty offense. The law was written, of course, to protect kidnap victims—to let their abductors know that if they hurt their prisoners in any way they could face execution. But just what constituted kidnapping was still a legal swamp, even after the law was rewritten in 1951.

At least one California Supreme Court justice agreed with me. As I turned to that court's reply to Wein's appeal—usually the first thing I looked at in a clemency file, since it summarized all the important facts and issues in the case—I saw that the court had voted six to one against Wein, and that Jesse Carter had been the sole dissenter. Carter had already granted Chessman two stays of execution because of his strong feelings against PC 209 as a death-penalty offense, and in the Wein case he spelled out his feelings in great detail.

"The majority has misconstrued the meaning of the word 'kidnaps' as it is used in section 209," Carter wrote in his dissenting opinion. Also, "The term 'carries away' is so ambiguous within the context of section 209 as to be meaningless. . . ." He listed Wein's crimes in detail, calling them "perverse and outrageous," deserving of severe punishment and little mercy. But to sentence him to death for these crimes, Carter wrote, "is excessive to the point of barbarity. . . .

"Consider the precise acts for which this court is affirming the death penalty," Carter continued. "Defendant seized and bound the hands of victim C.F. She told him where her money was but he took none. He helped her onto a bed four or five feet away and forced her to perform sex acts. He was clearly guilty of rape and perversion. The penalty for rape is not less than three years in the

94

state prison. For perversion it is not more than fifteen years in the state prison or less than one year in the county jail. These were brutal and revolting acts. But for moving C.F. four or five feet, 'helping' her to the bed, he is to be executed. Without this movement he would not have received the death penalty! The case involving U.H. is similar except that he did not rape her. Defendant committed the same atrocities on A.H. as he did on C.F., and in fact did more harm to her than to U.H. But in attacking A.H. he merely threw her to the floor and raped her and committed perversion. His penalty for this was not death, but two prison terms! Why? Because he did not move her the necessary *one inch* nor incidentally ask for her money! Of the condemned movements one must ask: What difference did they make? The answer: None."

Carter had eloquently summed up my own doubts about 209, doubts which weighed so heavily during the Chessman case. Then he went on to make an even more telling point. "In each of the other three situations involving the death penalty, if the victim had not been moved a few feet there would be no death penalty possible," he wrote. "Under the rule of this case a robber who shoves his victim against a wall is eligible for the gas chamber if a prosecutor arbitrarily chooses to ask for that penalty. Essentially section 209 may be used by a zealous prosecutor to kill one who has committed other more socially condemned crimes which carry less severe penalties.

"The instant case is the archetype. The deputy district attorney prosecuting Wein did this overtly. In his summation he demanded the death penalty not for the defendant's moving his victims but for the sexual assaults he made upon them. He cited the military law which inflicts the death penalty for rape. He belabored the lecherous acts allegedly done to victim L.S., then said, 'If this is not treatment which earns the defendant the extreme penalty of death, I never saw any. There is not a red-blooded man on this jury, there isn't a respectable woman on this jury who in my opinion would say otherwise.' "

What Carter was saying was obviously true. J. Miller Leavy had done the same thing here as he had in the original Chessman trial—turned a loophole in a badly written law into a noose with which to condemn a guilty man. I could never say this in public or in print, of course, without doing even more damage to my standing in law-enforcement circles, but the feeling definitely affected the decision I was about to make.

I looked through the other documents in the Wein file. Four new lawyers hired by his family argued at great length that the death penalty was excessive, that new evidence had surfaced casting doubts on Wein's guilt, that he had been badly defended and was mentally unstable if not legally insane. The new evidence was vague and unconvincing in the light of his victims' certainty of his guilt, and the issue of an inadequate defense had been dismissed by the California Supreme Court.

His mental history was of more interest to me. Wein had apparently consulted a psychiatrist in 1955, just before the first attack with which he was charged, and was diagnosed as being "psychotic or borderline psychotic." He had also attempted suicide by taking an overdose of Nembutol two weeks before his last attack in 1956; another psychiatrist diagnosed him as "severely mentally disturbed" at that point and transferred him to the Los Angeles County Hospital's psychopathic unit where he stayed for ten days before being allowed to sign himself out. There were also the usual conflicting tangle of psychiatric reports in Wein's file: two prison doctors said that while he was undoubtedly "sociopathic, antisocial, emotionally immature with psychoneurotic and psychosexual disturbances," he was definitely not legally insane. A private psychiatrist who examined him in prison reported, "He had an ambivalent attitude toward his wife, but he could not express his intense resentment directly toward her. He apparently directed his hostility toward other women." And another private consultant had this chilling prediction: "The repeated pattern of his crimes with the tendencies toward physical violence would make him a very dangerous type of sexual criminal who might very easily go on to crimes of greater violence."

Wein's file also contained about forty letters from friends of his family and business associates attesting to his character and asking for clemency. Against this I had to balance letters from five of his victims, begging that the death sentence be carried out. "I don't think I can ever sleep soundly until I know for sure that he is dead," one woman wrote.

The clemency hearing was held in my office on a Monday afternoon, four days before Wein's scheduled execution. While I listened carefully to everything that was said by Wein's lawyers and members of his family as well as representatives from the Los Angeles County district attorney's office, the truth is that I had already made up my mind. I was going to do for Eddie Wein what Caryl Chessman's previous felony convictions kept me from doing for him—commute his sentence to life without possibility of parole. In fact, I had already asked Cecil Poole to draft a memorandum showing how the Wein case differed from the Chessman case—the chief points being that Wein had no prior convictions and had never taken flight or tried to escape as Chessman did.

"I have given careful study to the case of Edward Simon Wein, who was condemned to death in 1957 in Los Angeles County for kidnapping, robbing and raping eight women and subjecting them to acts of sexual perversion," began the commutation document that I issued on June 4, 1959. "Five of these charges were kidnapping for the purpose of robbery with bodily harm, the harm consisting of the sexual offenses mentioned. . . .

"The record in this case shows sordid and outrageous assaults upon helpless women victims by a man who invaded their homes. Although the contention has been made that Wein is innocent, the evidence in this case overwhelmingly demonstrates, and I am personally convinced, that he is guilty of the offenses of which he is charged. I am also satisfied from careful study of the transcripts and the trial records, and from the invaluable information afforded me by the investigators of Attorney General Stanley Mosk, that the trial was fairly conducted and that the prosecution was vigorous, effective and honest.

"I am, however, dubious of the application in cases such as this of the kidnap statute pursuant to which the death penalty was decreed. The record here shows that each of the cases involved movement of the victim from one place within her home to another place within her home, and that although the distances involved varied from a few feet to seventy-five feet, in no case was the victim substantially moved from one place to another in the manner which we traditionally associate with kidnapping. I am aware that under the applicable statute, there is no restriction on the distance a victim must be moved in order to constitute a technical kidnapping; but I feel that only where there is a kidnapping in the true sense of the word, with bodily harm, should the death penalty be invoked.

"As heinous and revolting as Wein's crimes are, our Legislature has prescribed express penalties, falling short of the death penalty, for rape and sex perversion. Although the court's construction of Section 209 of the Penal Code is in my opinion amply justified by the language of that Section, I do not believe that the Legislature has clearly declared an intention to punish with death the kind of movement of the victim which is only incidental to the acts of rape or sex perversion, as distinguished from the kind of movement which we associate with the Little Lindbergh Kidnapping Law. . . .

"I have considered Wein's age, education and the circumstances which gave rise to the commission of these offenses. I am impressed with the fact that prior to these outrages he showed definite indication of psychopathic disturbances sufficient to require him to receive psychiatric examinations. I am also impressed with the fact that despite evidence of mental abnormalities he had not, prior to these offenses, ever been in any kind of trouble and had served honorably in the Armed Forces of his country.

"Although I respect highly the needs of law enforcement and the considered decisions of our court, I am left in grave doubt that this is truly a death case, and I am therefore compelled to resolve that doubt in favor of life. My own conscience tells me that in this specific instance the interests of justice and the best interest of the State of California will be served by granting to Edward Simon Wein a commutation of his sentence from death to life imprisonment without possibility of parole, and I hereby so act."

There was some small buzz of reaction over the next week or two: J. Miller Leavy condemned the commutation as "typical of the modern pattern of the Governor's actions," and other Los Angeles law-enforcement figures joined him in taking a free shot at me. But the general public didn't appear to be unduly upset, and the trickle of letters and cards coming to my office were about evenly split between praise and blame. Two years later, when one of Wein's lawyers filed a petition for a writ of habeas corpus so that the prisoner might be made eligible for parole at some future date, a few frightened people wrote to me in protest. "As the father of two young daughters, I implore you to do everything in your power to keep this man from ever being turned loose on society again," read one letter that I have in front of me now. I asked Cecil Poole to draft a reply, which said, "For your information, Wein is undergoing a sentence of life imprisonment without possibility of parole. No one can change this commutation except the Governor. Governor Brown has no intention of taking any further action whatsoever in this case. . . ."

And indeed I didn't—at the time. But five years later, as I prepared to leave office in 1966, the climate of justice had changed. Because of an order by the U.S. Supreme Court calling for retrials in the penalty phases of all capital-punishment cases under appeal, there had been no executions for almost three years. Eddie Wein had been behind bars for ten years, from all accounts a model prisoner, and friends of his family had written eloquent letters asking for further commutation. One former business colleague who had known Wein from childhood visited a prison psychiatrist and wrote me that the doctor "believes that if it were possible for Eddie to be paroled at some time in the future, there would never be any trouble with him because Eddie is considered smart and would now be able to conform to the outside world and support himself. . . . Considering the progress

Eddie has made, his mental health would improve tremendously should he be given the opportunity to be subject to or eligible for parole."

Perhaps the most persuasive petition came from Fred Dickson, who had succeeded Clinton Duffy as chairman of the Adult Authority, the agency in charge of parole supervision. It was dated November 21, 1966, and I quote from it in detail now because of the impression it made on me at the time: "The above-identified inmate of San Quentin Prison, Edward Simon Wein, is hereby recommended for removal of his Life Imprisonment Without Possibility of Parole status. As Warden of San Quentin Prison for the 21 months of Mr. Wein's imprisonment on Death Row and four and one half years following the commutation of his death sentence, I familiarized myself with his case and learned to know him as an individual. . . .

"Mr. Wein is an intelligent man of 43 years of age. He served honorably in the United States Air Force in the European Theater during World War II. At San Quentin Prison, he was assigned to work as clerk for the Protestant chaplain for six years. He had a very good work record, and was reported to have assumed his responsibilities well. In February, 1966, he attempted to contravene correspondence regulations through a part-time chaplain. This culminated in a disciplinary action, and his transfer to a clerical assignment in the institutional parole office. He attends all services of the Jewish religion, and is the pianist for the congregation.

"Wein readily accepts responsibility for his crimes, stating that he pleaded not guilty because he was too ashamed to acknowledge them. He has become able to make a critical evaluation of his behavior pattern. . . ."

Dickson's favorable assessment was supported by reports from psychiatrists at San Quentin, who found Wein's mental condition "much improved" and "stable" and who raised no objections to future parole. So, in December 1966, I further commuted his sentence to life with the possibility of parole.

I left office on the last day of 1966 with some regrets, but Eddie

100

Wein wasn't one of them. As my clemency secretary John McInerny turned over our files to incoming Governor Ronald Reagan's newly appointed clemency secretary, Edwin M. Meese 3rd, I remember feeling that in spite of a few setbacks I had done a pretty fair job of balancing the twin causes of justice and mercy. Now it was time to move on, to earn a living for my family and see what other adventures the future held.

I'd been practicing law in Los Angeles for almost eight years when in November 1975 I boarded an airplane for one of my frequent trips to San Francisco. The man in the seat next to me was a stranger, but he obviously knew who I was. "Have you seen this?" he asked with what sounded like contempt, handing me the front page of that morning's *Los Angeles Times*. "Trademark and a Memory Jail Man," said the headline he was pointing to. I read with growing horror how Eddie Wein's luck had once again run out. . . .

"A unique 'trademark' which helped to almost send a convicted rapist to the gas chamber 19 years ago, plus the sharp memory of a retired police detective, has put Edward Simon Wein back in custody again—this time, on suspicion of murder," the story began. "For Wein, now 51, who was released on parole Sept. 16, 1974, after serving 17 years in prison for sexually assaulting at least six Los Angeles-area women, his arrest yesterday, like his capture in 1956, turned on a once-in-a-million happenstance. But, in both instances, it was his trademark—putting his victims off guard by pretending to have lost his watch stem—that made him stand out and assured that he would be remembered almost two decades later. . . ."

The *Times* story went on to tell how a former LAPD detective named Robert Wright, retired for just two months, went to the regular monthly lunch held by a group of police colleagues and heard the details of two disturbingly similar recent crimes in the area around Los Angeles International Airport. A fifty-two-year-old Westchester housewife had been found dead, bound hand and foot, stabbed several times with a sharp instrument, strangled and drowned in her bathtub. In the second case, a forty-year-old Palms woman had narrowly survived death when she was sexually attacked, bound, beaten and stabbed in the neck by a middle-aged man who had answered an ad which she had put up in a neighborhood supermarket, offering a bed for sale. Hearing this, something began to stir in Wright's memory, and when his fellow detective then said that the murdered woman had also recently advertised some furniture for sale on a supermarket bulletin board, a light went on. Although he hadn't personally worked on the Wein case, Wright recalled the details. "We had a case back in the fifties of a man who went to the houses of women who had placed newspaper classified ads for things to sell," he said. "I can't remember his name, but this guy had a way of getting physical control over the victims, by pretending to drop his watch stem. When the women bent over to help him look for it, he grabbed them from behind."

Wright's detective friend was amazed. "Hell, that's what the suspect did in the Palms case!" he told him. Together, they sent off a request to the Adult Authority, looking for a recent parolee who had used the watch-stem gambit. Back came a name—Eddie Wein, paroled in 1974, now living with relatives in Rancho Park, close to both Palms and Westchester. A witness had seen a man leave the home of the murdered woman and enter a car: his description matched Wein and a car he had borrowed. Wein was arrested that night, and booked on suspicion of murder. The next day, the Palms victim picked him out of a police lineup; charges of attempted murder, rape and sexual perversion were also filed.

I finished the story, including a short paragraph about my successive commutations of Wein's sentences that made his parole possible, and handed the paper back to my seatmate. He must have seen on my face the distress I was feeling, because he was silent for the rest of the short trip. As for myself, I was racked with guilt and doubt. I had made mistakes before—anybody who makes decisions as part of his job finds out later that some of them were wrong—but this one had cost a woman her life. I honestly think that if, at that moment, I could have somehow traded the lives of all twenty-three of the people whose death sentences I'd commuted for the life of that Westchester woman, I would have done so.

In the months ahead, I followed Wein's trial at Santa Monica Superior Court without talking much to anyone about my own thoughts and feelings. Perhaps subconsciously I was waiting for the moment when someone would rise up in court and accuse me, though that moment never came. I cringed as I read the surviving victim's testimony about how Wein had tried to suffocate her, stabbed her in the neck, dropped a heavy flower pot on her head and was about to drown her in her bathtub when he was frightened off by a noise outside. I was particularly moved by a comment from the prosecutor, Robert Altman, who said, "It was, with hindsight, a terrible mistake to parole this defendant. Eighteen years in prison did nothing to cure his compulsion to violently degrade women. His method of operation has remained remarkably the same—the only modification being that he will no longer allow his victims to remain alive. This defendant should never be released from prison. It would be a tragic mistake to ever assume that he is 'burned out' or too old to repeat his crimes." I wondered if the psychiatrists who had examined Wein and found him fit for parole, the friends and business colleagues who wrote to support him, were sharing my feelings of horror and guilt.

In June 1976, Wein was convicted on all counts. The death penalty not being in effect at that point because of the U.S. Supreme Court's action, he was sent back to prison for three successive life sentences. Judge Charles Woodmansee, echoing Altman's words, said, "The court does recommend to the Adult Authority that Eddie Simon Wein never again be released from confinement."

During the period of Wein's second trial, I found myself going back to the record of criminal justice during my administration for whatever consolation I could find. There were some success stories among the twenty-three men whose death sentences I had commuted, most of which I've already talked about in this book. There were also the 430 prisoners convicted of other than capital felony crimes to whom I granted rehabilitative pardons during my two terms. Of that number, only two had been returned to prison for new felonies; one more was a parole violator; and twenty-seven others were subsequently convicted of misdemeanor offenses such as drunkenness or disturbing the peace. It was an impressive record, one which people such as Chief Justice Earl Warren and Justice Arthur Goldberg of the U.S. Supreme Court praised as being worthy of study by other states, but it didn't wash away the mistake of letting a Wein go free.

Two more years passed, and then came that day in 1978 when John Crooker, the very first man whose death sentence I'd commuted, came to my office in Beverly Hills for a visit. One of the things we talked about was Eddie Wein. "I wish there was a way you could have asked me about him before you granted that second commutation," Crooker told me. "I would have warned you against it. The man was very sick, very dangerous, and I think any one of the prisoners could have told you that."

Crooker's comments stunned me into rare silence. The implications were at once obviously simple and subtly ironic. Here was a man whose life I had spared at least in part because of his intelligence and future potential, now out of prison and leading a useful life, telling me that he and other prisoners turned out to be better judges of the inner nature of another man whose life I'd spared—better judges than a governor, several psychiatrists and a host of other skilled professionals. It seemed to me then and ever since an almost perfect parable about the entire death-penalty dilemma.

Whenever a Charles Manson or a Sirhan Sirhan is brought up for parole, it scares a lot of people. The possibility that one of these years they might somehow slip through the cracks to freedom is, I'm convinced, what keeps people so strong in their support for the death penalty. In spite of court sanctions against the practice, prosecutors have historically been able to frighten jurors into voting for a death sentence by reminding them of the fact that there really is no such thing as a life sentence without possibility of parole—that a governor can one day commute and a parole board can another day free virtually any prisoner.

Even though California and twenty-eight other states have laws on the books allowing courts to sentence criminals to life without the possibility of parole, every prisoner knows that those laws have built-in escape hatches. Felons convicted under the California law before 1982, for example, automatically have their cases reviewed by the Board of Prison Terms, which can recommend clemency to the governor after twelve years. Those convicted after 1982 have to wait thirty years, but even that is a short enough period to legitimately frighten a large segment of the population.

Totally removing a governor's power to change a sentence from life without possibility of parole sounds like a denial of his right to be humane and compassionate, but I would suggest that it is more humane and compassionate than forcing him to constantly decide on the life or death of an individual. If we could guarantee that nobody who committed a capital crime would ever get out of prison, there would be much less demand for the death penalty. And all the energy and expense of deciding whether an Eddie Wein should live or die could instead be used to look more deeply and carefully into the broader issue of whether he indeed should ever be released back into society.

CHAPTER SIX

Ma Duncan and Other Lost Causes

The word was out: Pat Brown was soft on capital punishment. Opponents used it regularly as one more stick to knock me and my programs. Did it bother me? Not particularly. In fact, aside from the political damage, it gave me a considerable amount of pride to be on what I considered the right side of a moral issue. I even made jokes about it. Once, after I'd been duck hunting with Chief Justice Earl Warren, reporters asked me how we'd done. "The Chief Justice got five ducks and I got four," I told them. "I would have had five, but I commuted one."

But it's important here to underline the fact that, unlike the recent governor of New Mexico who was so opposed to the death penalty that he refused to let *anyone* be executed during his final months (and then had to live through a jailbreak in which a couple of his reprieved murderers terrorized his own neighborhood), I refused the clemency requests of thirty-six condemned prisoners during my eight years in office. Along with the most famous cases, Chessman and Lindsey, thirty-four others went to the gas chamber during my two terms. For each of them, no matter how hard I searched, I couldn't find a compelling reason to go against the judgment of the court and the law of the state. Some of those cases are worth considering in detail.

Elizabeth "Ma" Duncan, for example, emerged from my own past to write a script that no Hollywood producer would touch.

While I was still in private law practice in San Francisco, I bought an eight-unit apartment building on Hyde Street for $42,000. It was fully rented and I was making a nice profit on my investment. Then, shortly after I was elected district attorney in 1942, the police came to me and told me that there were two prostitutes working out of one of the apartments in my building. I was sure that the newspapers would find out about it and blow it up into a scandal, so in spite of the income I decided to sell the building. A real-estate broker said that he had a client named Mrs. Elizabeth Duncan who was ready to pay $75,000 for it—a ridiculously high price, but I wasn't about to argue. I opened escrow, but unfortunately Mrs. Duncan was unable to come up with the money. I never met her; finally the broker told me, "I think this woman is nuts; you'd better forget about her," and I sold the building for a more realistic $52,000. Then her name slipped back into the corners of my memory for sixteen years, until newspaper headlines brought it out front again with a bang.

"Mother-in-Law Charged with Murder for Hire," read a typical headline on the day after Christmas in 1958. Mrs. Elizabeth Duncan, a fifty-four-year-old widow living with her lawyer son Frank, thirty-seven, in Santa Barbara and who soon became "Ma" Duncan in the jaunty shorthand of the press, had been indicted along with Luis Moya and Augustine Baldonado for the murder of Olga Duncan the month before. According to the police, Mrs. Duncan had promised to pay the two men $6,000 if they took her son's pregnant wife to Mexico and killed her. Instead, Moya and Baldonado drove Olga to the nearby town of Ojai, where they beat and strangled her to death and buried her in a field. When they reported back to Mrs. Duncan, she paid them only $400 for their work. Not surprisingly, they both were strong witnesses for the prosecution when Mrs. Duncan came to trial.

The story which came out before and during that trial was as amazing as it was sad and sordid. It turned out that the matronly Mrs. Duncan had been married eleven times, the first time when she was fourteen years old. Some of the marriages were in fact never valid because they were entered into while she was still legally married to someone else, and several were to younger men, to whom Mrs. Duncan promised large sums of money— when it wasn't forthcoming, the marriages were annulled. From one of her husbands, she demanded and received child support by the ruse of sending a pregnant woman claiming to be Elizabeth Duncan to a doctor and getting a false affidavit of pregnancy. She had a total of five real children from all her marriages: one died from a brain hemorrhage, three others were turned over to adoption agencies. Thus, she lavished all her love and attention on her son Frank, working in bars, restaurants and stores to put him through college and law school. In 1953, she was convicted of running a house of prostitution in San Francisco— which might have been the reason she wanted to buy my apartment building.

Frank Duncan decided to open a law office in Santa Barbara in 1956. The next year, afraid that her son was going to move out and leave her, Elizabeth Duncan took an overdose of sleeping pills. While visiting his mother in the hospital, Frank met a nurse named Olga Kupczyk and began dating her. Mrs. Duncan objected violently and ordered Olga to stop seeing him. When the nurse told her she was going to marry Frank, Mrs. Duncan was heard to scream, "You'll never marry my son! I'll kill you first!"

Nevertheless, Frank Duncan and Olga Kupczyk were married in June 1958. They lived together at Olga's apartment for several weeks, but in August, Frank gave in to his mother's repeated harangues and moved back in with her. That same month, Elizabeth Duncan began asking some of her son's shadier clients if they knew of anyone who would like to earn a large sum of money by doing a quick and dirty job for her. She also recruited a man named Ralph Winterstein to go with her to Ventura County Superior Court, where with Winterstein claiming to be Frank

Duncan and Elizabeth saying she was Olga Duncan, they asked for and received a decree of annulment of their marriage.

But Olga had become pregnant, and Elizabeth sought a more drastic solution to her problem—someone who would kidnap her daughter-in-law, take her to Mexico, kill her and then pour lye over the body to prevent identification. In November 1958, her inquiries led her to Moya and Baldonado, a pair of small-time hoodlums who agreed to do the job for $6,000: half immediately after the killing and the other half in six months. Elizabeth Duncan gave them a cash advance of $175, which they spent on gloves, adhesive tape, car rental and bullets for a borrowed pistol.

At 11 P.M. on the night of November 18, Moya and Baldonado drove to Olga Duncan's apartment in Santa Barbara. Moya rang her bell and told Olga that Frank Duncan was downstairs in their car, unconscious after an accident. As she ran downstairs to help her husband, she was hit on the head with the pistol and dragged into the car. Although she was seven months pregnant, Olga fought so hard that her attackers had to stop the car and hit her repeatedly on the head—so hard and so often that they broke their gun. When the rented car began to act up, the killers abandoned their Mexico plan and drove instead into the hills toward Ojai. Olga was still fighting desperately for her life; Moya and Baldonado took turns strangling her and digging a grave in a grove of orange trees. Finally, at about 2 A.M., they finished their grisly work and went back to Elizabeth Duncan for payment. She complained about the sloppy job and the final proximity of Olga's grave, gave them another $400 and told them that was all the money she could raise at the moment.

Olga Duncan's body was discovered two days later, and it didn't take the police long to pick up Moya and Baldonado—who admitted their guilt and quickly implicated Mrs. Elizabeth Duncan. She denied their story, saying the pair were former clients of her son who had come to her threatening to kill him because of dissatisfaction with the way he had handled their cases; she swore she paid them the money to keep them from hurting Frank. A Santa Barbara district attorney grabbed some headlines by telling a local newspaper just before the trial that "this is exactly the kind of case that shows why it's important for California to keep the death penalty." Mrs. Duncan's lawyer tried repeatedly to shift her trial out of Ventura County on the grounds that this statement had made it impossible for her to get an impartial jury, but the court turned him down. The trial began on February 24, 1959; Duncan entered pleas of not guilty and not guilty by reason of insanity. In addition to Moya and Baldonado, who had already pleaded guilty to first-degree murder, the prosecution brought on witness after witness to tell about Elizabeth's unhealthy fixation on her son, her repeated death threats to Olga, and her attempts to recruit other killers. On March 16, the jury came back with a verdict of guilty of murder in the first degree. Four days later, after hearing reports from court-appointed psychiatrists, Mrs. Duncan's insanity plea was rejected and a sentence of death was pronounced for all three defendants.

By the last week of July 1962, when appeals for clemency for Luis Moya, Augustine Baldonado and Elizabeth Duncan arrived on my desk, they had already squeaked by two prior execution dates as a result of stays from federal courts. August 8 was their next appointment with the gas chamber, and this time I was their only chance. There wasn't much to say in favor or defense of Moya or Baldonado: both were career criminals who had committed a particularly brutal murder of a pregnant woman for money. But Elizabeth Duncan was something else: a tormented woman whose path had once crossed mine.

The fact that she was a woman—the only woman sentenced to die during my terms as governor, and only the fifth woman ever sentenced to death in California history—did have some effect on my thoughts and feelings. I felt a great repugnance about letting a woman die, as I suspect even the toughest death-penalty advocate would. Our past personal connection, as fleeting and insubstantial as it was, did make me think about her as more than just a convicted criminal. This was something I tried to do in every clemency situation, to give the subject human dimensions outside the parameters of his crime, but I wasn't always successful.

As usual, my clemency secretary—in this case, Arthur Alarcon—had succinctly summed up the case and included all the relevant psychiatric evidence. "From a clinical psychiatric standpoint there is no evidence of mental illness, and she can best be fitted into the category of character behavior neurosis, which is relatively synonymous to a sociopathic personality," one doctor had written. Another said, "In the opinion of the undersigned, she is neither legally insane nor psychologically psychotic. The diagnostic impression is that the patient is suffering from a long-standing personality disorder, more specifically identifiable as a dyssocial reaction." The electroencephalogram we ordered was diagnosed as "mildly abnormal, but with no real clinical significance."

Alarcon concluded his report with these comments: "The district attorney's conduct in this case in making public statements prior to trial concerning the guilt of Mrs. Duncan and her co-defendants and his opinion that this case proved the necessity for the retention of capital punishment disturbed many prosecutors and other lawyers throughout California. However, the Supreme Court unanimously affirmed this case, in an opinion written by the Chief Justice, and held that the district attorney's conduct did not result in the denial of due process and the right to a fair trial.

"After reading the facts of this horrible crime involving the brutal murder of a pregnant woman who was seven months along, I am convinced that if this case were tried ten years from now and the venue were changed to New Hampshire, the same penalty would be recommended by the jury. In other words, the district attorney needlessly overprosecuted his case.

"There is no question that Mrs. Duncan is a bizarre woman with an unhealthy love for her son and abnormal thought processes. However, every psychiatrist who has examined her could find no evidence of psychosis or mental illness in the legal sense sufficient to justify a commutation or an act of clemency in this matter."

I walked into Alarcon's office with his report in my hand. "So you don't think the lady is crazy?" I asked. "Well, she's not your average baby-sitter," he conceded. "But that's not the question, is it? People who kill in ways that make a jury sentence them to death are not normal people, by and large. And you certainly can't commute her and let the other two die—it's all or nothing."

Arthur was right, of course. Elizabeth Duncan was as guilty of the savage murder of Olga Duncan as Luis Moya and Augustine Baldonado were—even more, in that she had brought about the crime by hiring them to commit it. In spite of the fact that she was a woman, a mother, a person with whom I'd once had some peripheral contact, I knew that there was a time in all capital cases when I had to just let it go, move on to other things. I was the head of a growing state, in need of new schools and public health programs, with an election coming up in a few months. I had to say to myself, "I've got lots of *good* people to take care of; I can't worry about this bad one anymore." And that's the hardest thing about running a state where the death penalty is part of the law—to be forced to think in those terms.

If the death penalty deters any kind of crime at all (and in the literally hundreds of studies I've read over the last forty years, I must say that I've never found any convincing evidence that it does), it should be the crime of murder committed while carrying a loaded gun during a robbery. That was a message I always tried to make very clear: take a loaded gun along on a robbery that results in a death and you'll go to the gas chamber for sure. Charley Luther Pike was carrying a loaded automatic pistol when he held up a Los Angeles auto parts store in 1960—his third armed robbery of the day. One of the customers was an off-duty policeman, and when Pike saw the handcuffs on his belt, he shot him down in cold blood. He also tried to kill the policeman's partner, waiting outside in the parking lot, and probably would have succeeded if his gun hadn't jammed.

Pike had three prior felony convictions, a record of robbery and violence going back to his time in the U.S. Army, and was diagnosed as being a sociopath but not legally insane. When his appeal for clemency reached my desk, there was nothing I could or would do to save him. Nor would I act to spare the life of Harold

112

Arlen Spencer, who in 1962 shot a Los Angeles cab driver in the back of the head while robbing him of four dollars. Spencer's lawyers argued that he was just a small-time car thief who had never hurt anyone before, but to my mind he sealed his fate when he slipped those bullets into his gun and set out to commit a crime.

The case of Lawrence Jackson had frightening echoes of the Eddie Simon Wein tragedy, although it happened over a shorter time period. The thirty-four-year-old Jackson was released from Folsom Prison on September 11, 1961, after serving a nine-year sentence for assaulting and raping several young women. His method was to call up women who had advertised for jobs in the "Situations Wanted" columns of newspapers and lure them into his car with offers of nonexistent positions. Four days after his release, while staying with his mother and an aunt in their Los Angeles home, Jackson called a woman who had advertised for a secretarial position, picked her up at her Hollywood apartment, drove her to a remote part of Riverside County where he'd worked on a fire crew while in prison, fractured her skull with a rock and then committed an act of forcible sexual intercourse while she was dead or dying. He was arrested the next day when he drove back to the area where he'd left the body.

Jackson's clemency file was a sad testimony to the inadequacy of our jail system in dealing with certain types of sexual offenders. He had first been arrested for rape in 1946, when he was nineteen, served less than a year and a half in prison, was released in 1948 and almost immediately began the series of assaults that would send him back behind bars in 1952. A psychiatric examination characterized Jackson as a "sexual psychopath" but also made a point of saying that he was "not mentally ill in the medical or legal sense." His lawyers argued that the state had failed twice to cure Lawrence Jackson, and that to kill him now because of that failure was clearly a cruel and unusual punishment. I saw the point of their argument, and might even have agreed if it weren't for the vision of that woman's battered body out in Riverside County. The possibility of that happening again finally made me turn down Jackson's request for clemency.

One factor that isn't often mentioned in discussions of the death penalty is a governor's responsibility for the safety of the staff and other prisoners in an institution where a particularly dangerous criminal might be incarcerated. When twenty-one-year-old Paul Eugene La Vergne was arrested for killing a San Diego cab driver during a robbery in January 1965, it turned out that he had been in trouble with the law since he was twelve years old. His record showed that he had managed to cram into a relatively short period a truly stupefying number of arrests for robbery, escapes from prisons, misguided paroles and their virtually immediate violations. Several times while in custody—at Youth Authority camps and at Soledad Prison—he assaulted other prisoners, on racial or sexual grounds, each time being stopped just short of inflicting severe bodily harm if not death. The murder for which he was sentenced to the gas chamber wasn't with a gun: La Vergne had brutally beaten the elderly cab driver and then strangled him with his bare hands. Once again, psychiatric examinations diagnosed him as having a "sociopathic personality disturbance; anti-social reaction but without psychosis." According to the clemency report, La Vergne had even been involved in an attempted assault since his arrival on Death Row. Keeping this dangerous and violent man from hurting a guard or a fellow prisoner played a large part in my decision to deny him clemency.

I often used the issue of disparity of sentence to keep someone from the gas chamber. As I'll discuss in more detail in the next chapter, if two men committed the same crime but for reasons of age or attitude or even sheer chance were given different sentences, the unfairness alone seemed to me to be reason enough to commute. But on some occasions the responsibility for the crime was so clearly on the shoulders of one man that it overrode the disparity issue. Dovie Carl Mathis and Billy Clyde Still were both charged with robbing and beating to death their friend Vernon Ray in San Jose in October 1963. It was Still who spotted Ray flashing a large bankroll in a bar and told Mathis about it; and when Mathis phoned Ray, told him his car had broken down and asked to be picked up, Still went along with the planned robbery. He hit Ray over the head with a tire iron while Mathis blinded him with a flashlight. But Still's blow was a light one; Ray was able to grab the tire iron and run away. Mathis and Still chased him; Mathis knocked Ray to the ground and hit him with a rock. Still removed the semiconscious man's money and was about to leave when Mathis said that he would have to kill Ray because he could identify him. Still protested mildly, then turned away and let Mathis finish off the victim with a rock—testifying later that he did this because he was afraid of what Mathis might do to him.

After their arrest, Still became a cooperative witness, leading police through the crime scene and admitting his share of the guilt. Mathis first tried to blame the killing on another man, Larry Jones, and then attempted to make Still look like the primary aggressor. Both men were found guilty of first-degree murder, but jurors during the penalty phase of the trial showed their belief in Still's story by sentencing him to life imprisonment and giving Mathis the death penalty. A major factor in their decision had been the twenty-nine-year-old Mathis's record: three prior convictions for violent assault.

Troubled by the disparity in sentencing, I reviewed Mathis's clemency report carefully. The trial judge had submitted a carefully reasoned letter explaining why he did not reduce the jury's verdict; it was obvious, he said, that Mathis "throughout his lifetime pursued a career of violence." He was out on bail on another charge of assault with intent to murder when he killed Ray, the judge reminded me. Both the prosecutor and the chief of detectives for San Jose wrote letters about the condemned man's lack of regard for human life. On the evidence contained in the report, I couldn't help but agree; I turned down Mathis's request for clemency.

* * *

Murders for hire, especially those involving organized crime, always presented me with problems in weighing clemency. Who should be the most severely punished, the "brains" behind the murder plot who often is miles away when the actual killing occurs, or the hit men who dumbly carry out his bloody orders? Joseph Rosoto was a smart crook originally from an immigrant family in Seattle who headed up a robbery ring which preyed on restaurants and nightclubs in the Los Angeles/Orange County area. After masterminding a series of successful stickups in 1956 and 1957, Rosoto decided to go along with four other members of his gang as they knocked over a night spot called the South Seas in Anaheim in March 1957. The others had their faces covered, but Rosoto's only disguise was a dark cap. Not surprisingly, his was the only face later picked out of police mug books by the nightclub's owner and his wife.

Rosoto fled to Seattle and tried his damnedest to avoid extradition to California, even staging an automobile crash to injure himself badly enough to require hospitalization. But he was eventually brought to Anaheim, where in a preliminary hearing in January 1959, the owner of the South Seas and his wife formally identified him as one of the men who had robbed them. Rosoto made bail and was out on the street awaiting his trial when in the early morning hours of February 7, the nightclub owner and his wife were cut down by a series of shotgun blasts as they were returning home. The man died almost instantly from massive chest wounds; his wife had her hand blasted off and the other arm badly mutilated, but she survived. A large man was seen running from the area, and five shotgun shells were found in the yard.

At first, it seemed that Joe Rosoto had the perfect alibi: he was on an airplane bound for Seattle at the precise moment the shots were fired. One of his henchmen, John Vlahovich, had driven him to the airport, and both men had made sure that they would be noticed by talking loudly in the airport bar, asking dumb questions of various airline personnel, and other similar tactics. Rosoto eventually beat the South Seas robbery rap, but he and his gang couldn't leave well enough alone. Back in Seattle, Rosoto, Vlahovich and another man named Donald Franklin took

116

to bragging in front of anyone who would listen about how they had silenced a witness in California and had gotten clean away with it. They threatened anyone who crossed them with the same treatment. Eventually, Rosoto's half-brother—who had helped set up the automobile-accident scam and now wanted his share of the insurance money—was threatened; he then cooperated with police and helped bring about the arrest in Southern California of Rosoto, Vlahovich and Franklin on murder charges.

The three men were tried and found guilty in September 1960, and the jury took just under three hours to recommend the death penalty for each. Two years later, I had to decide on clemency for any or all of them. Rosoto's lawyers argued that whatever Vlahovich and Franklin might have done, their client clearly couldn't have been involved in the actual shooting, being airborne at the time. Attorneys for Vlahovich and Franklin said they were mere dupes, blindly following the orders of the man who paid their wages. I couldn't swallow either story, and thinking of that murdered man and the woman who had her hand blasted away I refused to take any action.

But not all murders for hire were as clear-cut. Allen Ditson was a slight, soft-spoken intellectual who owned and operated a jewelry store and watch-repair shop in North Hollywood. He was also known to buy and repair wrecked cars, and to deal in exotic weapons on occasion. But his primary occupation was as head of a gang of highly organized armed robbers. It was a gang in which each man had an assigned role carefully planned by Ditson; all its members knew that any deviation from that role, or any talking about the gang, if they were caught, could bring severe retribution.

Carlos Cisneros was twenty-four when he met Ditson and joined his gang, eventually working his way up to the post of Ditson's chief lieutenant. Cisneros was a much simpler soul, a young man raised in various foundling homes, who was married, with four children, and earning $85 a week in a factory job before he turned to crime.

During the robbery of a liquor store in November 1959, one of

the gang members—Robert Ward—failed to perform his assignment satisfactorily. He was supposed to tie up the couple who
owned the store, but the wife managed to free herself and then
her husband, who grabbed a gun and began firing. The robbers
were forced to flee, hiding the cashbox they'd stolen in a hedge.
When they went back to retrieve the box, Cisneros and fellow
gang member Eugene Bridgeford were arrested. Freed on bail,
they met with Ditson, who told them that in addition to his on-
the-job failure, Ward was also demanding money to keep quiet
about the gang's activities. "He's got to be taken care of," Ditson
said. "I want you to do it soon." He gave Cisneros a two-pound
jeweler's ring gauge with one end of its fourteen-inch length
wrapped in tape to use as a weapon.

Bridgeford and Cisneros drove to Ward's house, persuaded
Ward to join them in his car for a drink from the two pints of
whiskey they'd brought along, and then began an incredible
odyssey of errors that would be hilarious if they didn't involve a
man's death. Cisneros had left his weapon in his own car, so he
picked up a hammer from the floor and began hitting Ward with
it. Ward managed to get out of the car and leaned against a tree,
where Cisneros hit him again and with Bridgeford's help loaded
him into the trunk of their car and drove off. After a few minutes,
Ward began shouting for help from the trunk so loudly that
Cisneros had to turn the radio up to cover the noise. Then he
misjudged a turn, hitting a curb so hard that he blew a tire. But
the jack and the spare were in the trunk with the still-moaning
Ward, so Cisneros sent Bridgeford off to call Ditson and ask him
to bring a tire and jack. Ditson arrived with the necessary items,
the tire was replaced, and the men returned to Ditson's jewelry
store to plan their next move. Bridgeford, saying he wasn't feeling well, asked permission to go home. He would later plead
guilty to a lesser charge and serve as the chief prosecution witness against Ditson and Cisneros.

Ward was still making noise in the car and Ditson was worried
about the neighbors, so he took a .38 revolver and had Cisneros
drive him into the farther reaches of the San Fernando Valley

until they came to an isolated spot. When they opened the trunk, a bloodied Ward got out by himself and asked for a cigarette. Ditson shot him in the chest. Ward ran off; Ditson shot him again, this time in the back. "Give me another one," Ward groaned as he lay on the ground, so Ditson knelt beside him and fired one last shot into his head. After Cisneros dug a grave, Ditson took a butcher knife from the car and cut off Ward's head and his arms below the elbow—to prevent identification of the body, he told Cisneros.

Ward's severed head and arms then went on a six-month journey as bizarre as anything else in this strange case, being buried and dug up no fewer than three times and each time involving new witnesses who would eventually give evidence to the police or the FBI. When Ditson and Cisneros finally stood trial for Ward's murder in June 1960, Ditson denied doing the shooting or being the leader of any gang, although he did admit to burying Ward's head and arms in the desert. Cisneros at first agreed to take a polygraph examination and then tried to disown the incriminating results, saying he had been coerced into the test against his will. Both men were found guilty and sentenced to death.

Two years and several unsuccessful appeals later, Ditson and Cisneros turned to me for clemency. Arthur Alarcon strongly recommended against it in both cases, and due to the savage nature of the crime, I had to agree that Ditson certainly deserved no mercy: he had coldly planned and carried out the murder and dismemberment with no visible emotion or remorse. But I wasn't so sure about Cisneros: he seemed to be a simple, trusting man of low intelligence who was evidently a loving husband and father. I found in the record a written statement he had sent to the trial judge after his conviction: "I admitted what I did because I couldn't live with myself any more. I had terrible nightmares, going through what had happened that night over and over. I considered myself a monster, even dog's would run away from me where they never did before. . . . I was afraid to play with my kids because I might go craze and hurt them. . . . The way I feel about getting caught, is like a Blessing from heaven. Even though I find myself fighting fore my life, I feel clean and have a wonderful feeling inside. Getting all that out of my system is enough to make any body happy and that's the way I feel."

In those awkward words, I thought I saw the possibility of, if not redemption, at least remorse. I decided to commute Cisneros's sentence to life without the possibility of parole. Alarcon was in Los Angeles giving a speech when his secretary reached him with the news of my decision. "Since I had already written my report to support refusals to commute on both cases," Arthur recalls, "I had to quickly dictate a new version, giving the governor at least some possible grounds for commuting Cisneros. About a year later, after I became a federal judge, I was in a Mexican restaurant in Los Angeles when a very big Hispanic gentleman came up to me and said, 'I want to thank you for advising the governor not to kill my brother Carlos.' I decided not to tell him that I had originally advised *against* clemency. . . ."

Carlos Cisneros turned out to be a model prisoner, eventually becoming eligible for parole under a new law. In 1978, now a deeply religious man, he was returned to his family and took up a trade he'd learned in prison. He, too, paid me a visit at my law office, talked about his family, and made me feel that my decision was the right one.

CHAPTER SEVEN

Reasons to Commute

In spite of the continuing executions, and the fact that I was denying about half again as many requests for clemency as I was approving, in 1962 Richard Nixon attacked my perceived anti–capital-punishment stance when he ran against me; and Ronald Reagan made it a major issue in his 1966 campaign. I knew that I was a better governor for California than either of them, and I also knew that if I soft-pedaled the death-penalty issue I'd have a better chance of being reelected; the polls over the years showed the people of California in favor of the death penalty by a margin of at least 60 percent and sometimes as high as 70 percent. And yet I continued to go against public opinion in my search for reasons to commute death sentences. Why? Because I really was a bleeding-heart liberal who cared more about the criminals than their victims, a charge that's been leveled at all opponents of the death penalty? I don't think so. Reading those case reports filled me with as much anger against the killers as any man alive, but anger is a luxury that a governor can't afford. As the last stop on the road to the gas chamber, it was up to me to make sure that the law—even if it was one I disagreed with—was being fairly applied. And in many cases, underneath the terrible details of the crimes themselves and the justifiable anger they created, I found examples of unfairness and injustice that even the hardest heart couldn't ignore.

Milo Smith was a colorful and well-known figure in the Los Angeles seaport suburb of San Pedro. By 1957, when he was fifty-five, the stocky and hard-drinking bachelor had been practicing criminal law for thirty years. He wore a flashy diamond ring and a gold watch and always carried large amounts of cash; his suite of offices on Pacific Avenue contained not only his law books but also an extensive wardrobe of suits, ties and about forty pairs of handmade shoes. There was also a huge old safe, reportedly stuffed with money, but Smith's eyesight had become so bad that even with his strong glasses he hadn't been able to work the dial for nine years and left the job to his secretary.

Milo Smith's body was found near that safe on the morning of August 27, 1957. He was lying on his back, with one of his own neckties knotted very tightly around his throat and another binding his hands beneath him. His suit coat and pants were off and thrown to one side, his billfold was empty on a worktable, his glasses were on a shelf some distance away. A small saucepan of water was sitting near the victim's head. The safe had blood on it, and there was a bloody footprint and kneeprint on the carpet near it. A souvenir rifle, broken in half, was near the body, as was a telephone with a broken receiver. Under the body was a small wooden gavel, also stained with blood.

When the police and the medical examiner arrived, they decided that Smith had been beaten to death sometime between 5 and 7 A.M. His entire rib cage was fractured; there were fifty-five separate wounds on his body; and the necktie around his neck had been pulled so tight that it fractured the hyoid bone. Missing, along with the money from Smith's billfold, were his watch and ring, a .45 automatic he kept in a desk drawer, and four pairs of shoes. The safe appeared not to have been opened.

It didn't take long to reconstruct Milo Smith's last night. He had been drinking heavily in some of his favorite San Pedro bars, first with his secretary and later with the son of a client. At about 2 A.M., Smith and his companion met two young black men on the street, twenty-two-year-old Charles Evan Turville, Jr., and seventeen-year-old Lamar Mitchell. Smith gave Turville a twenty-dollar bill from his roll and sent him off to buy a bottle of whiskey. Turville came back and said he couldn't find an open liquor store; he tried to return the money to Smith but the lawyer insisted he keep it. Then the four men got into Smith's car and drove to his office. Smith made a point of taking Turville and Mitchell on a guided tour of the premises, showing off his clothes and his collection of shoes. When Mitchell said his feet were the same size, Smith made him a present of several pairs of shoes. Then Smith called a cab driver he knew, who brought over a bottle of whiskey but declined an offer to stay for a drink. At about 3 A.M., the son of Smith's client left, driving Smith's car; Smith called the man's mother at 3:30 A.M. and arranged to pick up his car in the morning. At 4:57 A.M., a local cab company received a call from Smith, asking that a cab be sent to his office. The cab was dispatched, but the driver came back empty, saying that he couldn't find anyone at the address. Another call came at 5:20 A.M., from someone other than Smith, and this time the cab driver honked his horn, got out of his cab and entered the building. Standing outside the door to Smith's office, he heard the sound of drawers being opened and shut, but when he knocked, the noise stopped and nobody answered. The driver stumbled over several pairs of shoes at the foot of the stairs. As he got back into his cab, he noticed someone watching him from Smith's window, and he was certain it wasn't the stocky white lawyer.

Putting together all the evidence, the police quickly identified Turville, a Navy veteran originally from Pittsfield, Massachusetts, recently laid off as a marine machinist at a San Pedro shipyard, and Mitchell, a local high school dropout. Two days after the crime, Turville was arrested by the FBI in Brooklyn, New York, at the home of an aunt. He was wearing Milo Smith's watch and ring, and at first he insisted that the lawyer had given them to him. But as they began to question him in detail, Turville

123

broke down, led the agents to his luggage, which contained his bloody clothes and Smith's gun, and then gave them a full confession. He told how he and Mitchell went into the rest room in Smith's office and decided to rob him of the money he had on his person as well as what was in the safe. They both grabbed the lawyer, forced him to the floor and ordered him to open the safe. When he refused, they tied him up and took turns hitting him with judo chops to the body. When Smith tried to crawl away, Mitchell hit him over the head with the souvenir rifle. When the lawyer lapsed into unconsciousness, Turville revived him by bathing his head with a wet cloth. He also beat Smith about the legs with a wooden gavel he found on his desk. But he swore that the man was not dead when they finally left after finding the combination in his wallet and trying without success to open the safe themselves.

Los Angeles police arrested Lamar Mitchell at his home the next night. They found ninety dollars in cash in his wallet, and two hundred-dollar bills that he had tried to hide in the waistband of his trousers. Mitchell's initial explanation was that he had won the money playing pool. Then, when detectives showed him a report from a New York newspaper about Turville's confession, he changed his story—admitting that he had gone with Turville to Smith's office but insisting that the beating of the lawyer was all Turville's work. A jury didn't believe him; both defendants were found guilty of murder in the first degree, in the course of a robbery. Because of his age, less than eighteen at the time of the crime, under California law Mitchell could only be sentenced to life without possibility of parole. Turville got the death penalty, and by the time his appeal for clemency reached my desk in September 1959, he had exhausted all his legal challenges.

As Cecil Poole pointed out in his clemency report, the killing of Milo Smith was certainly one of the most vicious we had ever seen, and I searched through the records for some clue as to why Turville had behaved so violently. He had been raised in a respectable family; his intelligence was above average and he had good verbal skills; he got into some minor trouble in high school but seemed to have straightened himself out by joining the Navy. Examiners did find that he had been involved in a long list of serious accidents ever since childhood: falls from trees, crashes on motorcycles, a stabbing during a fight at a party. But Turville's psychiatric evaluation indicated no brain damage and showed him to be only marginally emotionally disturbed—certainly not insane. Excessive drinking didn't seem to be a defense factor: although Smith's blood alcohol level showed him to be legally drunk when he died, both Turville and Mitchell made a point of saying they'd had just two small drinks apiece with the victim and nothing before.

Two things bothered me about the case. Why did Milo Smith invite two young men he had never met before to his office in the middle of the night? Was it just an act of drunken camaraderie, or was it—as the defense tried belatedly to suggest, without any supporting evidence—for homosexual purposes? In neither event did this take anything away from the horrible nature of the crime, but it was still a puzzle and could have affected the sentencing phase.

More importantly, I was deeply troubled by the disparity of the sentences given the two equally guilty defendants. True, as Cecil Poole pointed out, "a review of the record indicates clearly that had it the power the jury undoubtedly would also have sentenced Mitchell to death," and both the California and the U.S. supreme courts had rejected the charge of unfairness raised by Turville's lawyers. But, as usual, I was trying to move beyond legal limits as I looked for reasons to commute.

Cecil and I talked about the case for a long time. He felt strongly that Turville had been hurt by his defense team's attempts to cloud the issue—first by trying to show that his confession to the FBI was given under duress and then by raising the specter of Smith's homosexual intentions. "The trial judge appears to have become quite impatient with Turville and his counsel for what were manifestly dishonest representations," Poole pointed out. I agreed: some of this might have rubbed off on the

125

jury. Cecil wasn't as bothered as I was by the disparity of sentencing, but he was troubled as to just why Smith had invited Turville
and Mitchell up to his office.

In the end, I decided to use both points as my reason to
commute. "There is no substantial issue in my mind either of
guilt or of the fairness of the trial," I wrote in the commutation
document. "I am impressed however that this is a most unique
case. The victim himself inexplicably accosted these young defendants, brought them to his office, gave them drinks and im-
portuned them to remain while he displayed and talked of his
wealth. Neither the robbery nor the fatal assault were planned
beforehand, and the record is clear that the idea was not in their
minds until virtually implanted there by the victim himself. Far
from planning robbery, the record is undisputed that Turville
earlier had tried to return Smith's money to him. Although the
felony-murder rule of this State takes no account of the fact that
the death in this case was unintended, the peculiar surrounding
circumstances here present may properly be considered in determining whether executive clemency, in the limited form of commutation from death to life, should be imposed. I have
considered too the fact that Mitchell, no less culpable than his
co-defendant, was by law spared the death penalty because of his
age, while Turville, five years his senior and with no felony record
whatsoever, received the death penalty. I have therefore concluded in the circumstances that equal justice warrants a commutation of Charles Evan Turville, Jr.'s sentence from death to
confinement for life without possibility of parole. . . ."

I should add here, not as evidence of any particular insight on
my part but for the record, that Turville—like several others
whose sentence was commuted to life without parole—eventually did get out of prison because of changing laws. The last I
heard he was leading an exemplary life.

Drinking and unplanned murder also played a part in the case of
Stanley Fitzgerald, but I spared his life for reasons of geography.

Fitzgerald was an amiable man of thirty-four who sold cars and

126

farm equipment for a living. He was a bachelor, and spent most of his spare time and money in bars near his San Francisco home. One night in August 1960, in such a bar, he overheard two men—M. J. Young and George Bonn—talking about wanting to go to Reno to gamble. Fitzgerald joined the conversation and offered to drive them to Nevada. They left the next morning, in a car which Fitzgerald had borrowed from a friend. Several bottles of whiskey and a .22 target pistol were part of their luggage for the trip.

A few miles east of the town of Truckee, Fitzgerald turned off the main road, saying that he wanted to stop at the farm of a man who was interested in buying a tractor, but he couldn't find the place, so the three men drove around many side roads, drinking whiskey and shooting the pistol at trees as they went. At some point, they finally stopped, finished off the whiskey and decided to go for a swim. Fitzgerald got into a drunken fight with the other two men, was hit on the back of the head with a bottle hard enough to stun him but not knock him out, began firing the pistol and killed Bonn while wounding Young in the arm. When he saw Bonn lying dead on the ground, Fitzgerald was so filled with remorse and revulsion that he gave the gun to Young and begged him to kill him. Young didn't, but instead apparently helped cook up a story about he and Bonn being held up by two men to cover the killing and give Fitzgerald a chance to escape. Fitzgerald took Bonn's watch and wallet, drove to the Reno airport, cashed two checks made out to Young, and flew first to Oakland and then to Portland, Oregon. But Young, under questioning by the Nevada County sheriff, soon broke down and told the true story. Fitzgerald was arrested in Portland and brought back to Nevada City for trial.

It was the biggest thing to happen in the small mountain community since Humphrey Bogart and Ida Lupino filmed the movie *High Sierra* there twenty years before. Nobody could remember the last time a real murderer had been lodged in the Nevada County Jail, and when a few town drunks decided to break out of their cells and take Fitzgerald with them, the level of

127

excitement rose to near-hysteria. All the prisoners were quickly recaptured by a posse of rifle-toting townspeople, some of whom were in court a few days later when Fitzgerald's trial began.

After listening to Young's testimony and hearing an account of a confession which Fitzgerald made to the Nevada County sheriff, the jury took just three hours to find the defendant guilty of murder in the first degree—in the course of an armed robbery— and agreed with the prosecutor that the penalty should be death. Several courts turned down Fitzgerald's claims that there was no intent to rob, and that his confession was merely an admission of the facts in the case. So once again, in 1962, I became the final voice on whether or not a man should die in the gas chamber.

Although Arthur Alarcon made no direct recommendation in his clemency report, his usual yardstick—the equal geographic distribution of justice—seemed to support a commutation. Had this same crime occurred in Los Angeles or San Francisco, Arthur pointed out, it almost certainly would not have been tried as a first-degree murder case. Another factor was the recent jailbreak, which had whipped up public reaction against Fitzgerald. I had pretty much made up my mind to commute his sentence anyway, and what Arthur told me the night before the clemency hearing clinched it. "I just had a visit from the Nevada County prosecutor," Arthur said. "He told me that he couldn't admit it in public because it would kill him politically, but Fitzgerald doesn't deserve to die. He said that if he thought the jury would vote for the death penalty he never would have asked for it in the first place. But he also said that if you or I mentioned his visit at the hearing, he'd deny ever having been here."

Sure enough, when I asked the prosecutor at Fitzgerald's clemency hearing the following morning if he had any second thoughts about the death sentence, he said that he did not. Arthur and I agreed to keep his secret, and have done so until this moment. Ever since then, his behavior—and ours—has seemed to me to sum up society's incredibly mixed feelings about mercy and justice and the death penalty.

*　　*　　*

I've already said that my inclination was to deny clemency in a case where a loaded gun was used during a robbery. When John Deptula beat a man to death with a bowling pin in 1961, the choice of weapons prompted me to commute his sentence.

Deptula was a big, simple-minded, shambling man of forty-three who worked as a day manager of a bowling alley in Los Angeles. One night, after drinking a lot of beer, losing $200 in a card game and needing money to pay his rent, he decided to burglarize the alley where he worked. He knew that the night manager, Al Mosser, was usually asleep by about 3 A.M., so he waited until 5:30 A.M. and used his keys to let himself in. Sure enough, Mosser was dozing in a chair inside the small office. But as Deptula headed toward the safe, Mosser stirred. Deptula panicked, went to the rack where the bowling pins were kept, retrieved a pin and hit Mosser over the head with it. When he continued to stir, Deptula hit him several more times. Then he opened the safe, took out the $1,760 inside, wiped the bowling pin clean and returned it to its rack. Deptula then took Mosser's body back to his apartment and hid it in a trunk.

The next morning, Deptula showed up for work at the usual 9 A.M., called the owner of the bowling alley and told him that the safe was open and empty and Al Mosser was nowhere to be found. They both told the police that the usually trustworthy Mosser must have either robbed the safe himself or was forced to do so against his will.

Two weeks later, police called by a sanitation worker found a dismembered body in a pit toilet at a recreation area in San Gabriel Canyon. The body was subsequently identified as Mosser's, and with it were the moneybags from the bowling alley safe. Under routine questioning, John Deptula broke down and confessed. He entered a guilty plea, waived a jury trial and because the murder was committed during a burglary was sentenced to death. A year later, I was called on to decide Deptula's fate.

It didn't take me long to make up my mind to commute. The crime itself was a nasty one, but I could not find any of the premeditation I thought necessary for first-degree murder. If Deptula had brought along a gun or even a knife, I probably would have let him die, but he didn't go into that bowling alley with a weapon of any kind. In the end, I didn't see how killing this man could possibly deter anyone else from reaching out in the height of panic for whatever heavy object was handy and ending a life with it.

There seemed to be no reason at all to commute William Lee Harrison's death sentence: he was a violent man with a violent past. But a hunch persuaded me to give him a sixty-day stay of execution, and then Fate stepped in to make my decision easier.

Harrison had been menacing women almost all his adult life. Something smoldering within this usually soft-spoken man seemed to burst into flames during sexual situations. He stabbed a girlfriend in the back in a jealous rage, attacked another woman in a bar, beat his ex-wife and threatened her with a shotgun. Then, in December 1961, when Harrison was forty-nine, he stabbed and slashed to death the twenty-four-year-old woman he'd been living with, Mrs. Doris Martin, on a street in Berkeley and tried to do the same to her mother.

Harrison and Mrs. Martin had been living together for three years, along with her nine-year-old son, but in November, a fight had sent her back to stay with her mother. A month later, the couple had one of their periodic verbal battles on the telephone, this one ended by Mrs. Martin's mother grabbing the phone and threatening to call the police. When the two women and the boy prepared to go out to a church function, waiting in the street outside was Harrison, armed with a large hunting knife. He leaped upon Mrs. Martin, inflicting fourteen severe wounds, and when her mother came to her aid, he slashed the older woman about the face and ear and threatened to kill her, too. Then, as neighbors and onlookers called the police, Harrison walked off, still carrying the bloody knife. He was arrested three blocks away. One of the police officers told him that Mrs. Martin was dead; Harrison said he'd meant to kill her and hoped he "got the other one, too." Then he begged the officers to go ahead and shoot him: "What do I have to do to make you shoot me?"

Harrison was charged with murder in the first degree, because he had been lying in wait outside the apartment, and assault with intent to murder. He pleaded not guilty, claiming that he had "blacked out" during the attacks, but the jury deliberated for just over four hours and convicted him on both counts. During the penalty phase, the prosecution presented a damning dossier of Harrison's violent history, including testimony from his ex-wife and a former woman friend, both of whom had been the victims of his rage. They also introduced evidence that thirty-two men who had previously been convicted of first-degree murder and sentenced to life in prison were currently out on parole in Alameda and Contra Costa counties, the areas closest to the scene of the crime. The jury seemed to get the message: after ten and a half hours of deliberation, it sentenced Harrison to death.

Lawyers for the defendant raised several issues during his automatic appeals, including their feeling that the "lying in wait" doctrine of first-degree murder had been wrongly applied since Harrison had rushed over to Mrs. Martin's apartment immediately after their argument on the telephone and had therefore acted in the heat of passion. But the court held that witnesses had seen Harrison waiting around outside for long enough to justify the charge. Harrison's appeals were rejected and his execution date was set for September 1963.

I was out of the state when Harrison's request for clemency reached the governor's office. Acting Governor Glenn Anderson, a loyal Democrat and a declared foe of capital punishment in charge during my absence, read John McInerny's report recommending against commutation. "What would the governor do?" he asked. John told him there was no way to be sure, but on the evidence he thought I would agree with his recommendation. Anderson, however, was bothered enough by the issues of premeditation, lying in wait and the heat of passion to ask for more information—including details of previous cases involving the killing of husbands or wives by their mates. John found him fourteen cases in the last fifteen years of men who were executed for killing their wives, ex-wives or common-law wives, the most recent case that of Vernon Atchley, which I discussed earlier. As McInerny pointed out to Anderson, my first decision in that case had been to deny clemency. Only when Arthur Alarcon found evidence of serious brain damage did I decide to commute Atchley's sentence.

Under these guidelines, Anderson decided to let Harrison's execution proceed as scheduled. But when I returned just before the execution and quickly read through the report, I was troubled; something told me to do more digging. So I gave Harrison a sixty-day stay, during which two important things happened. First, I got a letter from one of his jurors, who felt on reflection that he and his fellow panelists had been unduly frightened into voting for the death penalty by the specter of Harrison someday being allowed out of prison. Then, while I was mulling that over, the head physician at San Quentin reported that Harrison had liver cancer and would be dead in six months. All things considered, I felt that we had found sufficient grounds to commute. I let John McInerny explain to Glenn Anderson why we had changed our minds, and John reported back that he *thought* Anderson believed he wasn't being sandbagged. As for William Lee Harrison, cancer soon took the life that I was reluctant to charge to the already overloaded account of the State of California.

The case of Norman Whitehorn also involved some extra digging and second-guessing by my clemency secretary. The fact that my decision had to be made during a period of national anguish added to the dramatic tension.

Whitehorn was twenty-five, an intelligent but deeply troubled young man who had already served a four-year prison term for forcible rape and had recently been acquitted on a similar charge. Actively bisexual since his prison days, he was working at his brother-in-law's restaurant in Los Angeles when he met an eighteen-year-old U.S. Marine named Charles Hummel and began a relationship with him. In the early morning hours of Easter Sunday, April 22, 1962, Whitehorn and Hummel were drinking in a Hollywood night club, where they became friendly with Mrs. Angela Gums, a thirty-seven-year-old divorcée. When Mrs. Gums mentioned wanting to call a cab to take her home, Whitehorn offered to drive her in his car. The three drove into the Hollywood Hills, where Mrs. Gums was raped twice by Whitehorn, strangled with a necktie and thrown into a ravine.

Whitehorn and Hummel then drove back to Whitehorn's apartment, cleaned themselves up and went out to an amusement park in Long Beach, where they had earlier agreed to meet two young women. Whitehorn tried to force one of the women to have sex with him and threatened her when she refused, but the women managed to persuade him to leave. That night, Hummel returned to his base at Twentynine Palms, near Palm Springs, and Whitehorn went back to his restaurant job.

Five days later, overcome with remorse, Hummel confessed to his base chaplain that he had been involved in a serious crime. The first version of his statement made him out to be merely an observer of the rapes and the murder. Under further questioning by the police, however, and mostly during interview sessions which he requested, Hummel changed his story no fewer than five times, each time adding details of his involvement in the murder of Mrs. Gums.

By contrast, Whitehorn's statements changed very little from the time he was arrested. "Whatever happens, I'm going to be eliminated from society," he told his questioners, admitting his part in the rape of Mrs. Gums but denying that he had strangled her.

When both defendants took the stand during their trial in August 1962, the teenaged Marine with no prior criminal record came across in a much more positive manner than the older, more case-hardened ex-convict. Hummel and Whitehorn were each found guilty of first-degree murder, but at the end of the penalty phase—when testimony about Whitehorn's prior convictions and other evidence of rape or attempted rape had been heard—Hummel received a life sentence, while Whitehorn was given the death penalty.

Whitehorn based his automatic appeals on two main issues:

whether or not the jury had been correctly instructed that Hummel's changing statements could only be used as evidence against Hummel and not Whitehorn; and whether evidence of his prior rape convictions should have been allowed. The courts ruled against him on both counts, and his execution date was set for December 3, 1963. You may remember those turbulent days—less than two weeks before, John F. Kennedy had been killed in Dallas. I had flown to Washington for the funeral, and John McInerny put together his clemency report on Whitehorn for a hearing to be held in Los Angeles on my return.

The report listed the sordid facts of Whitehorn's life: the oldest child of a couple whose heavy drinking and sexual promiscuity split the family when he was nine, he had been in some sort of sexual revolt ever since his teens. Dishonorably discharged from the Air Force because of his rape conviction, he had had a failed marriage, marked by violence, and a series of failed jobs. Only the repeated kindness of his younger sister and her husband, who owned a restaurant, kept him employed. The same psychiatrists who testified that Charles Hummel was sane and rehabilitable because he had openly talked to them found Whitehorn sullen and unwilling to communicate.

McInerny had recommended that I deny clemency in this case, and I saw no reason to disagree. I announced my decision and went back to the sad business of mourning one president and trying to help another keep the country together.

"Looking back on it, the Whitehorn case was one where I really earned my money," John said recently. "While I was preparing the report, a little voice in the back of my mind kept saying that there was something wrong here, something missing. But I didn't know what it was. On the basis of the information we had, Whitehorn was a loser with no redeeming social qualities. I recommended against clemency; we held the hearing; Pat agreed with me; that was that. But the voice continued to nag at me, so I went back through the original copies of all the statements made by Hummel and Whitehorn. Whitehorn had always denied strangling the woman at all, while Hummel kept adding more and more details of his involvement in the killing. Then I found what had been bothering me: Hummel's final admission, made voluntarily just before his trial, was that he alone had strangled the woman as she sat naked on Whitehorn's lap in the front seat of the car.

"The climate in the country wasn't exactly conducive to mercy or clemency, but I showed the governor the evidence of injustice—the man who'd actually done the killing getting a life sentence while his companion got the death penalty—and suggested that he might want to look at the case again, maybe give Whitehorn a sixty-day stay. 'No,' Pat said when he saw what I had. 'I'm going to commute him right now.' And so he did."

Some crimes were so terrible that I could fully understand and sympathize with the judges and juries who sentenced those who committed them to death. But during the clemency process, I had a different kind of decision to make, and other things to consider in addition to the crime itself. The facts in the case of Charles Golston were particularly repellent: the twenty-year-old window cleaner broke into a home in Long Beach in August 1961, raped a seventy-nine-year-old woman, choked her when she screamed for help, and continued to rape and strangle her to death even when he saw the police arrive outside.

The officers who arrested him, the prosecutors who charged him and the judge who tried and convicted him were still convinced, two years after the crime, that Golston deserved to die. "The defendant did not plead insanity, nor intoxication, nor a drugged condition at the time of the offense," the trial judge reminded me. "It was vicious, cold-blooded, and without any excuse whatsoever. He was unquestionably guilty of first degree murder . . . it is only fair and just that he pay the extreme penalty for his outrageous conduct."

The prosecutor wrote, "It requires an extremely cold individual to enter a residence during the night when the occupant is on the premises. It also requires an especially depraved individual to sexually attack a 79-year-old woman. . . ." And the Long Beach police pointed out that "at no time during the investigation did he show remorse for the acts which he had committed but was calm and nonchalant at all times."

On the face of it, Charles Golston was as undeserving of clemency as anyone who had ever applied to me for it. Then I began to read further in the report begun by Arthur Alarcon and finished by John McInerny. "In summary, we have here a dull Negro youth who was reared in rural Oklahoma within a rejecting, unloving home situation," said a social evaluation by a Corrections Department counselor. "Although he seemed to be a conforming, well-adjusted boy, he was experiencing a great deal of psychosexual disturbance. His aberrant sexual behavior—stealing female undergarments from clotheslines and cutting them up—went unnoticed. . . . Other than his sexual confusion, the subject was plodding along as well as can be expected with his limited potentials in trying to meet his social obligations."

I also read for the first time Golston's own account of the crime: how he had meant to have sex with the victim's daughter, a fifty-two-year-old woman who lived in the same building and had given him some encouragement along those lines, but entered the wrong apartment by mistake. "The victim, when awakened, became startled and began to scream," the counselor's report said. "He states that he got scared and just raped her. He doesn't know why he had to rape her. He was attempting to leave but apparently someone called the police. In order to prevent the victim from screaming, he intended to tie the pillow case around her mouth. He mistakenly strangled her because the pillow case slipped to her neck."

I had been a prosecutor long enough to know that statements made by criminals after the fact are notoriously unreliable, tinged with wishful thinking and belated regret, but there was something in Golston's words that had a small ring of truth. He had no previous criminal record, had worked hard ever since he was thirteen, and seemed from all accounts to be genuinely bewildered by his crime. "He willingly describes at length and in detail the circumstances surrounding his offense, giving the impression that by doing so he might possibly come to understand it," a psychological evaluation told me.

Letters in the file from prison chaplains and guards described Golston as likable, quiet, mild-mannered, well behaved, presenting no disciplinary problems. I put the report down and wondered who Charles Golston really was—the vicious, cold-blooded, depraved character described by the judge, the prosecutor and the police, or the baffled, troubled individual pictured by the prison authorities? There was no way to erase from my mind the image of his victim and her final agony, but I also knew that subjecting Golston to similar agony would neither bring her back nor deter any other sexual time bombs from exploding.

I called John McInerny in and told him I had decided to grant Golston a commutation; I wanted him to draft the document and spell out the reasons I'd outlined. John argued against it for a long time, then said, "Governor, I just can't do it." At that point, I exploded. "You're not the governor!" I shouted. "*I'm* the governor! Go write the damned report!" John remembers going back to his office so angry that he was about to cry. "It was the hardest document I ever had to write," he recalls. "Finally, I wrote it, took it back and shoved it in front of Pat's nose. He read it, and the first thing he said was, 'See, I told you the guy should have been commuted to begin with!' Then he stopped smiling and said, 'John, I know how hard that was for you to do. Thank you very much.' I went back to my office, and this time I really *was* crying."

When I heard about Earnest Leroy Jacobson, who drowned his twenty-one-month-old daughter in 1964, my first feeling was also one of basic, elemental horror. Nevertheless, the clemency process helped find a man behind the monster and provided me with reason enough to commute his sentence.

Jacobson was a chronic alcoholic who had been in trouble most of his adult life. In 1948, at age eighteen, he left school to join the U.S. Navy and get away from a drunken, brutal father. His first hitch went smoothly, but after he reenlisted in 1951, Jacobson began to drink heavily himself. Court-martialed eight times for drunkenness and unauthorized absences, he was dishonorably discharged from the Navy in 1956. The next year, he was arrested for stealing a car and received a suspended sentence. Hospitalized several times for alcoholism, beginning in 1958, he was released as improved each time—and each time resumed his heavy drinking almost immediately. In 1961, he threatened his wife with a butcher knife and spent thirty days in jail on an assault charge. The following year, he menaced a cab driver with a stolen pistol, and also threatened to kill his wife, their baby daughter and his wife's boyfriend. The cab driver was able to summon help and disarm Jacobson: he spent ninety days in jail this time, with three years on probation. A prison psychologist diagnosed him as being on the verge of a schizophrenic breakdown and recommended that he be committed to a mental hospital before he became dangerous to himself or society. Her advice was not taken.

It was at this point in his life that Jacobson met Mrs. Grace Babcock, a divorced mother of three. Newly divorced himself, he moved in with Mrs. Babcock and her children; their daughter, Kelly, was born in April 1962. By now Jacobson was incapable of holding a job, so while Mrs. Babcock went to work in a factory each day to supplement their welfare payments, and the older children went to school, he stayed home in their apartment in Signal Hill, south of Los Angeles, drinking almost constantly but looking after the baby with what witnesses described as love and tenderness.

At about 2 P.M. on January 23, 1964, Jacobson called a county welfare social worker and said he had just killed his child. "I need twenty dollars to buy cigarettes in jail," he told the social worker. When the police arrived, the doors to the Babcock residence were locked. They found Jacobson sitting in a neighbor's front room. They asked him what he had done, and he at first answered, "Nothing." When they asked him to open his door, he began to put candy and cigarettes into his pockets. "I'm going to need these in jail," he explained as he got up. The officers later said that neither his speech nor his movements appeared to be impaired by alcohol.

Inside his own home, Jacobson told the officers they would find his daughter Kelly in the bedroom where he'd put her. He said he had taken the sleeping child and drowned her in the bathtub; he added that her death was painless. In the bedroom, they found the child lying dead on the bed, fully clothed in damp garments and covered with a blanket. They noticed that the front of Jacobson's pants and shirt were also still damp. The baby deserved to die, he told the officers, "because she was a little bastard," a remark he repeated several times during the course of his subsequent questioning. He also asked for something to drink, saying that he had been drinking beer steadily since eight-thirty that morning but that his supply had run out. According to the police, he showed no remorse for what he had done.

Jacobson's court-appointed lawyer entered a plea of not guilty by reason of insanity, seeking to prove that his drinking history had affected his mental condition. Mrs. Babcock and her children testified that Jacobson deeply loved the little girl he'd killed, and that he had been drinking constantly for several days before the crime. They also testified—to counteract police evidence that Jacobson didn't appear to be drunk when he was arrested—that no matter how much he drank, it rarely showed in his ability to walk or talk. But the jury disregarded the psychiatric testimony, finding Earnest Jacobson sane and guilty of murder in the first degree. After further deliberation, the jury sentenced him to death.

By the time the case reached me for clemency consideration, in late November 1966, I had lost my job to Ronald Reagan—who had used my stand on capital punishment against me very successfully—and I was trying to finish up my last months in as useful and orderly a fashion as possible. As I've said, my first reaction to the crime was one of revulsion: it seemed outside the bounds of human sympathy or compassion. The trial judge, although he was a supporter of my own views on the abolition of capital punishment, made a point of saying that he felt the death penalty was justified here because of the helplessness of the infant victim and what he called "the complete lack of worth in Jacobson's past life." I was inclined to agree until I began to read the report prepared by John McInerny, in many ways the toughest of my three clemency secretaries.

"I would recommend, based on a complete review of this file, that the death sentence of Mr. Jacobson be commuted to one of life without possibility of parole," John wrote. "Jacobson committed a particularly brutal and senseless crime—the murder of a helpless child. The crime cannot be justified; it can only be partially excused by the fact that it was committed in a semi-alcoholic stupor. If vengeance were the primary purpose of our legal system, the present death penalty would be richly deserved.

"Jacobson is not, however, a dangerous man if kept confined away from access to liquor. A sentence of life without possibility of parole will adequately ensure the protection of the public, and yet would punish Jacobson in adequate measure. Such punishment, in my opinion, will best serve the best interests of justice in this case."

There was a short note at the end of McInerny's report: "Justice Stanley Mosk of the California Supreme Court, who wrote the majority opinion against Jacobson, called me informally and stated that while he thought the decision of the Court was legally correct, he also felt that Jacobson was a confirmed alcoholic and mentally ill. He feels that a commutation would probably be proper."

I had used Mosk's opinion as the final reason to commute John Crooker in my first clemency case almost eight years before. Now I used his, and John McInerny's, as my justification for commuting Earnest Jacobson's sentence to life without possibility of parole.

CHAPTER EIGHT

The Final Sixty-four—
and the Chosen Four

The story by Wallace Turner in the *New York Times* on the day before Christmas, 1966, summed it up: "Governor Edmund G. Brown, an outspoken foe of capital punishment, has the lives of 64 men in his hands these last few days before he leaves office. It appears they weigh heavily.

"Yesterday, Mr. Brown's executive secretary said he hesitated to intrude on the Governor's 'inner doubts and thoughts' as he ponders for the last time the question that has been a nightmare haunting him for eight years in office. There are 64 condemned murderers in the San Quentin prison. This is a record number for the state. . . .

"The Democratic Governor has been under pressures from many sources since his defeat by Ronald Reagan, the Republican candidate, in November. There are indications that the pressure Mr. Brown feels most is the one urging him to commute all death sentences to life in prison. A strong program urging him to make blanket commutations was mounted in November. This included a statement from the Most Reverend Joseph T. Mc-Gucken, Roman Catholic archbishop of San Francisco, urging the Catholic governor to act.

"On Wednesday, Governor-elect Reagan announced the appointment of his clemency secretary—Edwin Meese 3rd, a deputy district attorney in Alameda County. The announcement held an ominous note for the opponents of capital punishment. It said that Mr. Meese was 'a believer in capital punishment as a deterrent to crime'—a view that Mr. Reagan has said was his own. . . .

"A persistent report has circulated from Sacramento in the last few days that Governor Brown was considering whether to issue blanket reprieves of a year or more to permit the State Legislature time to once again consider a bill ending capital punishment. Mr. Brown was not available for comment on this. . . . But he said a few days ago that 'I have decided that I am not going to commute all 64 as I have been asked to do by some groups.' To grant a blanket clemency would be to place himself above the laws of the state that provide for death penalties, Governor Brown said.

"He has been getting up at 5 A.M. to review the papers on each condemned prisoner, to decide which he feels are justifiable cases for clemency."

It's true that the pressure on me to make some parting gesture against capital punishment was great—pressure from church groups and other opponents and also from inside that part of me which felt that whatever I'd done over the years hadn't really changed anything. And from a life spent listening to priests and other clergy I did at least give the appearance of taking in what they said. But it's also true that I never seriously considered giving blanket reprieves or commutations to all sixty-four men on Death Row. I had been elected twice by a majority of the people of California in a pact or trust to uphold their constitution and their laws, and I wasn't about to break that pact or violate that trust now that a few hundred thousand votes had shifted the other way. So I studied the files of the sixty-four condemned prisoners and came up with four whom I thought deserved commutation.

* * *

142

William Earl Cotter, Jr., was an unremarkable young man of twenty-three, an unemployed factory worker who shared a house in the Los Angeles suburb of Bellflower with an elderly couple, Ben and Elizabeth Buus. Cotter paid $43 a month for his part of the house, $8 of which went to the Buuses for gas and electricity, and was known to be a quiet and courteous tenant. In October 1963, Cotter was several days late with the rent because, he said, his unemployment check hadn't arrived.

At about four-thirty on the afternoon of October 15, Ben Buus left his house through the kitchen door to help a neighbor with a chore; his wife was in the front room playing the organ. He came back about twenty minutes later to find the kitchen door locked. Buus knocked and got no reply; he was taking out his key when he saw Cotter coming toward him from the bedroom. Cotter unlocked the door, then stepped back; Buus saw that he was holding a knife. "Don't move or I will get you," Cotter said. "I got your wife."

Buus heard his wife moan and ran around the house to the front door, shouting for help. He found his wife facedown in the kitchen, bleeding profusely. A neighbor, answering Buus's shout, saw Cotter running away down the street. At Buus's request, this neighbor called for an ambulance and the police. Then he joined Buus in trying to help his wife, who was gradually losing consciousness, and who would die later that night as a result of twenty-six stab wounds.

Police who answered the neighbor's call found several drawers open in the bedroom, but Ben Buus told them that nothing appeared to be missing. He also gave them a description of Cotter and repeated what he had said at the kitchen door. The police set off to look for Cotter, but within minutes they received a radio message that he had called the station, given his name, said that he had just tried to kill a woman, wanted to give himself up and would wait by the telephone booth until the police arrived.

Cotter was taken into custody quietly; he admitted stabbing Elizabeth Buus and handed over the weapon he'd used, a folding knife that was open in his pocket. During several questioning sessions, he told essentially the same story: how he had planned to rob the elderly couple but not hurt them because they'd always been kind to him; how he came to the Buus's front door under the pretext of wanting to pay his rent; how Mrs. Buus had begun to scream when he showed her the knife and asked where she kept her money; how, although he didn't know why, he had stabbed her when she screamed and continued to stab her after she fell to the floor.

The prosecution based its case for first-degree murder on two things: intent to commit robbery, as shown by the evidence of the opened drawers in the Buus bedroom; and premeditation, because Cotter had entered the house with his knife open in his hand. The jury accepted both arguments, found Cotter guilty of murder in the first degree and in the subsequent penalty phase sentenced him to death.

Cotter had not yet officially requested clemency when I reviewed his case, so I had no formal report to use as my guide. But reading through the trial transcripts made me wonder about his intent. Was murder really in his mind when he rang the front door bell that afternoon? Nothing in his ordinary, working-class background indicated a capacity for violence: he had no criminal record of any kind. Did the fact that he had an opened knife in his hand mean he planned to kill with it? Or was it more an issue of a closed pocket knife not really being enough of a threat to make anyone turn over their valuables?

Once again, a terrible crime had been committed; an elderly woman had been deprived of her life and her husband had been deprived of her company. But I was after justice, not retribution. Nothing I could do would restore that woman's life. If Cotter had used a gun, I probably would have let him die. But I couldn't see how sending him to the gas chamber would deter some future frightened would-be robber from panicking and striking out at his victim with his hand and whatever happened to be in it. I commuted Cotter's sentence to life without the possibility of parole.

* * *

Leo Lookado was so mentally retarded that killing him would have been—as one of his teachers said—"like sending a ten-year-old to the gas chamber." With an IQ of 65, Leo was barely above the level of an idiot. Yet this twenty-year-old man had been supporting himself, his sixteen-year-old wife Norma Ann and their two baby daughters by working as a farm laborer in the Modesto area of the San Joaquin Valley. And the only trouble he had ever been in before was truancy—skipping the special education classes that even at their lowest level were too hard for him to understand.

Lookado was like the character Lennie in John Steinbeck's *Of Mice and Men:* big, strong, slow and basically gentle. Norma Ann had been only fourteen when they were married and was not ready for the responsibilities of motherhood, so it was Leo who did most of the household chores and looked after the babies, in addition to his farm work. One Sunday in October 1964, Leo got up at 5 A.M., took his .22 rifle and said he was going hunting. When he returned a few hours later, he seemed upset and there was blood on his shirt. Tossing sixty dollars in small bills on the bed, Lookado announced, "I just shot old John down at the Shell station." Norma Ann thought he was trying to get her attention to make up for an argument about money they'd had the night before, so she ignored him. And even when she learned that John Inman, who owned a gas station in Modesto, had indeed been found dead on his floor that morning—his body riddled with bullets and then set on fire—Norma Ann kept quiet for months about what Leo had said.

Lookado was arrested on a traffic charge in Bakersfield in February 1965, and because the police found his .22 rifle hidden under a seat in his car, they sent for a deputy from Modesto who began to question him about the gas station killing. The usual cautions about having the right to remain silent and having an attorney present were given, but Leo was frightened, knew no lawyers and asked instead for permission to call his mother. The police told him it was up to him to decide whether or not to call a lawyer; nobody else could decide for him. Leo then asked to call his wife and his father, and these requests were also parried. Finally, as the questioning continued, Lookado broke down and told his story. On that October morning, he had gone down to Inman's station. He was the first customer; he and Inman chatted, and Leo purchased a dollar's worth of gas and a quart of oil. When Inman went inside the station to make change, Lookado followed with his rifle. "This is a stickup," he announced. "I need to get some money." When Inman moved toward him, Leo shot him six times, hit him over the head with the rifle, then poured a can of gasoline over Inman's body, took the money from the cash register and dropped a lighted match on the body.

Lookado waived a jury trial and entered a plea of not guilty by reason of insanity, but two court-appointed psychiatrists testified that although he was seriously retarded, he was still legally sane. Leo's confession, and a statement about the crime he later made to a cellmate, were enough to convince the trial judge that he was guilty of first-degree murder and deserved the death penalty.

Like Cotter, Lookado had not yet formally requested a clemency hearing, so I had to rely on the voluminous trial and appeal transcripts as I reviewed the case in those waning hours of 1966. There I found an interesting exchange between the trial judge and Leo's court-appointed lawyer on the question of premeditation—whether or not Lookado planned in advance to kill Inman. "This defendant is mentally a child," his lawyer argued. "He is not capable of planning that far ahead. . . . His mental age is well under eighteen, the age at which a person may be executed in this state. I realize that the law refers to chronological age, but nevertheless this defendant's mental age should have some bearing upon his criminal responsibility at least insofar as something so grave as capital penalty is involved."

The judge contended that by arriving so early at Inman's station, Lookado had deliberately worked out a plan where he wouldn't be stopped by other customers. "If you look at the total scheme and the thing that was done, it's obvious to me that it was done with deliberation and calculation," he said.

But the lawyer was convincing when he argued that Lookado's lack of intelligence made him choose a place near his home, a place where he was well known. "I can truthfully say with no attempt at sarcasm or humor that only a moron would have committed a robbery of this nature," he said. "A person of any-where near adequate intelligence, if he were so criminally in-clined and wanted to rob a gas station, could have easily robbed a hundred others in the area where he wasn't known, with an equal chance of getting the same amount of money. And I might add that only a person of subnormal childish mentality would have made the confessions that this man made to a fellow pris-oner. . . ."

Lookado's appeal hinged largely on whether or not he had been deprived of his right to counsel when the police talked him out of calling his mother, wife and father. Six of the judges of the California Supreme Court said that he hadn't, but Justice Ray-mond Peters's dissent made a good point. "Looking at the inter-rogation in its entirety, as we are required to do," he wrote, "the conclusion is inevitable that the confession here involved was secured by evasion and artifice. . . . The denial of the right to counsel by evasion or neglect of the suspect's request to counsel constitutes no less a Constitutional violation than a denial by explicit rejection."

But in the end my decision to commute Leo Lookado's sen-tence to life without parole didn't have a lot to do with the finer points of the law. I looked at the letters in his file from his former teachers and other educators who worked with the mentally retarded—especially the one who said that killing him would be like killing a child. I studied the reports of the psychologists who had visited Leo in prison: they found him baffled and frightened about what he had done and what would happen to him. "I are very much afraid. . ." began one of his unfinished letters to Norma Ann. Whatever the death penalty was intended to achieve, I knew that it wasn't to purge the world of mental cripples like this.

The last two men whose sentences I commuted, Clyde Bates and Manuel Chavez, were involved in a crime so horrible and so newsworthy that even today people who are old enough can remember at least its vague outlines. Bates and Chavez also made headlines when they took part in an attempted prison break from Death Row in 1962. Nevertheless, their death sentences had bothered me from the moment I took office, and as I was leaving, I was finally able to do something about them.

The Mecca Cafe in the area just south of downtown Los Angeles was a sleazy bar where frequent fights were part of the floor show. So when four very drunken men arrived at about nine-thirty on an April night in 1957 and three of them almost immediately got into a brawl, nobody was surprised. One of the four, Oscar Brenhaug, was so drunk that he went right to the bar and sat there in a stupor. The other three—Bates, Chavez and Manuel Hernandez—tried to persuade a couple of women customers to dance with them. When they were refused, the men cursed the women in extremely foul and graphic terms—causing a bartender and another male customer to take exception and begin the physical process that resulted in the ejection of Bates, Chavez, Hernandez and the stuporous Brenhaug from the premises. As they were leaving, the three more coherent ejectees made loud threats of vengeance and retribution.

Driving around the downtown area, their brains boiling with rage and alcohol, Bates, Chavez and Hernandez came up with a terrible plan for their revenge. They picked up a five-gallon bucket, filled it at a gas station, then drove back to the Mecca Cafe, where they double-parked with the engine running and left Hernandez in the driver's seat. Bates took the bucket of gasoline; Chavez had several books of matches. When Brenhaug muttered some query or protest, he was firmly shoved back into the car and told to shut up.

At the door to the Mecca, Bates shouted something and hurled the bucket of gasoline into the bar. Chavez lit a book of matches and tossed it in on top of the spilled fuel. The resulting fire was rapid and lethal: in less than five minutes six people sitting at the bar were burned to death and two more were critically injured.

Bates and Chavez ran back to the car, joined their two waiting companions and drove off. While Brenhaug slept in the vehicle, the other three men spent the rest of the night drinking beer in another downtown bar until it closed. Using license-plate information given to them by witnesses, police found and arrested Bates and Brenhaug at Bates's home shortly after 3 A.M. Chavez was picked up the following afternoon, and Hernandez was arrested the day after that. During the subsequent hours of questioning, Brenhaug and Hernandez generally admitted their roles in the crime, but Bates and Chavez steadfastly denied any involvement in the fire. Brenhaug became a witness for the prosecution and the case against him was dropped; the other three were charged with six counts each of first-degree murder under two separate special circumstances—murder committed during arson and murder committed during torture for the purpose of revenge.

The trial lasted two months: neither Bates nor Chavez testified, but Hernandez took the stand and made such a convincing show of mostly being along for the ride that in August 1957 the jury gave him life in prison without parole. Bates, a thirty-six-year-old burglar, car thief and chronic alcoholic employed most recently as a sign painter, and Chavez, a twenty-five-year-old truck driver with a juvenile record, were both sentenced to death. Appeals and writs got them past three execution dates, but by July 2, 1962, the pressure must have become too much for them to bear. That day, they joined with four other men on San Quentin's Death Row in a desperate but doomed escape plan. Cutting their way out of their cells with shop tools, they disarmed two guards and took them hostage. Then they called Warden Fred Dickson and threatened to kill the guards if their demands for safe passage weren't met. Warden Dickson stalled them until reinforcements arrived, then persuaded the prisoners to free the hostages and return to custody.

Because of the ruling by the U.S. Supreme Court that forced retrials in the penalty phases of most pending capital cases, Bates and Chavez were still among the sixty-four men on Death Row as my second term ended. John McInerny's report on the two prisoners was unusually long and detailed as he recommended against clemency. "This was a horrible crime. Six human beings were killed in the fire and two more were seriously injured," he wrote. "Neither man has ever admitted his guilt nor shown any particular remorse for his crime. Both men were active participants in a subsequent attempted prison break during which they assaulted two guards and threatened to kill them. Letters from Warden Dickson indicate that in his opinion Chavez is 'considered to be potentially very dangerous' and Bates is 'a very dangerous individual.' In my opinion, based on their past actions, their defiant attitude and their lack of remorse for their crimes, if either is commuted he will constitute a constant serious threat to the lives and safety of custodial officers and prison officials. . . ."

What John said was important and true, but I'd been thinking about the case longer than he had. I still keep among my papers a letter from a man in Long Beach, attached to a yellowed newspaper clipping, sent to me on April 7, 1957, while I was attorney general and had just asked for a moratorium on the death penalty because of the Burton Abbott fiasco. "I understand that you are against capital punishment," the letter said. "I enclose to you from the Long Beach Press-Telegram which may enlighten you on the subject."

Under the headline "Should We Get Rid of Death Penalty?" the newspaper ran an editorial that began, "Last Thursday night two men drove up in front of a cocktail lounge in south central Los Angeles. One of the men poured a large can of gasoline on the floor of the lounge. The other tossed in a match. They roared away—leaving six persons fatally burned. What should society do with these men, and others, who wantonly take the lives of their fellow men? Many persons, shocked and vengeful, would say that the punishment ought to fit the crime—that death should be the punishment for killing. Others, whose spokesmen testified in Sacramento last week at a hearing on a proposed abolition of capital punishment, would say the punishment, at worst, should be life imprisonment. The death penalty, they would say, is no deterrent to violent crime."

The editorial had already tipped its hand by using the words "at worst," lumping opponents of the death penalty in with people who were "soft on crime" and wanted shorter sentences for criminals of all kinds. From my experience, this is far from accurate: opposition to the death penalty is a deeply felt moral issue, not some offshoot of misguided liberalism. Still, I read it through, noting the old familiar arguments that supporters of capital punishment have used over the years, including the one that goes, "Sure, I can't *prove* that the death penalty has ever deterred a criminal, but who knows how many people faced with the prospect of the gas chamber or the electric chair think twice before committing a violent crime?" And I've kept the clipping handy ever since, mostly to remind me that the more things change, the more they remain the same.

In spite of John McInerny's sound reasoning, a few things bothered me about the Bates and Chavez case. One was the amount of drinking that had gone on in the hours leading up to the fire. Testimony differed, but it was clear to me that enough alcohol had been consumed that day to cloud the minds and judgments of everyone involved. This in itself was no excuse for a horrible crime, but it was one more mitigating factor in weighing the life-death decision. Even more important was the fact that Hernandez—who had helped plan the revenge and buy the gasoline—had been given life in prison because, by choice or chance, he had stayed with the car while the other two went into the Mecca Cafe. Should justice turn on such a creaky hinge as this?

There remained the important issue of the attempted jailbreak. As governor, I was as responsible for the safety of prison guards as I was for any other citizen. How could I convince this particularly beleaguered group of state employees that I had their best interests at heart if I commuted the sentences of two men who took guards as hostages and threatened to kill them? The answer was that in spite of seemingly having nothing to lose, Bates, Chavez and the other four condemned men *didn't* kill their hostages. This was the message I hoped to get across to other prisoners in similar situations: Don't harm your hostages and you have a chance to live.

There was one more hurdle to get over. Because Bates had several previous felony convictions, I needed the approval of the California Supreme Court to commute his sentence. So in the waning hours of the first Brown administration, I called Chief Justice Phil Gibson and asked for a reading on the court's willingness to act. He called me back surprisingly quickly. "They'll give you this one," he said. "But I think it's because they know you won't be able to ask for any more."

Clyde Bates and Manuel Chavez were removed from Death Row and assigned to other parts of the prison system. Bates put a few minor infractions on his record before changes in the law made him eligible for parole in the late 1970s; Chavez was generally well behaved. Both men were eventually returned to the outside world, where, to the best of my knowledge, they have caused no further trouble.

CHAPTER NINE

Adding It Up

When I was district attorney of San Francisco forty years ago, a couple of my friends in the police department gave me a present: a blue steel .32-caliber revolver that they'd taken from some criminal. In spite of the fact that I've since donated hundreds of hours and thousands of dollars to the cause of gun control, and in spite of my strong belief that the sale of handguns—the single greatest cause of crime in our society—should be severely curtailed if not banned outright, I still keep that gun, unloaded, in my bedside table. I have no idea where the bullets for it are or if they still work; I hid them someplace years ago when my children were little. I also have no idea what would happen if I decided to pull that gun out of its drawer in the event of a burglary, although I'm almost sure that the gun would once more find its way back into the criminal world.

I keep that gun for the same irrational and illogical reasons that thirty-seven states and the federal government keep the death penalty—as a kind of talisman against the dark forces that surround and threaten us all. I made my last official decision on the death penalty at the end of 1966, but I've been studying it and arguing about it ever since. It is one of those issues that seem to instantly polarize and divide us into enemy camps: abortion and gun control are others. Like those, the death penalty strikes deep chords of fear and guilt within the human soul; like those, it carries a load of emotional baggage that makes it hard to discuss, especially in the cool medium of print, without sounding pedantic or preachy.

In 1963 I made a second impassioned speech to the California legislature in support of another moratorium on the death penalty. Like my 1960 address, from which I quoted in Chapter Two, it didn't shift enough hearts or minds: the 1963 moratorium was also defeated in committee by eight votes to seven. But I'd like to include just a small section of that speech here as an introduction to some final thoughts:

"I recognize there is no clear consensus among us on the moral justice or injustice of capital punishment. Nor is there consensus on the compassion we should or should not feel for those who have died, and those who now await death, at our hands. For that reason, I will not center my present argument for a moratorium on the controversial grounds of public morality or pity for the lowest members of an imperfect society. Rather, I will confine my case to that which is not debatable in the light of reason and of historical knowledge:

"The failure of capital punishment to deter capital crime.

"The unjust and unpredictable enforcement of the death penalty in California."

At the beginning of this book, I asked somewhat ingenuously if those fifty-nine life-versus-death choices that had been forced on me as governor had made any difference. Obviously, they did to the twenty-three men whose lives I spared, and to their families. And although I was never able to convince enough legislators to carry through a moratorium on the death penalty, I'd like to think that my commutations kept the issue in the public eye vividly enough to stimulate the continuing debate. Even further, I hope that the climate of doubt that my decisions created helped influence first the California Supreme Court and then the U.S. Supreme Court to declare the death penalty unconstitutional after I left office. (It was Chief Justice Donald Wright of California's highest court who wrote the majority opinion in February 1972, thereby causing Governor Ronald Reagan to classify Wright's appointment as the biggest mistake he ever made.)

Since then, as I've noted, both courts have retracted or modified their decisions, and the death penalty is once again the law of the state. More than 230 condemned men fill San Quentin's Death Row facilities as I write these words in August 1988, with new arrivals being added every few weeks. Across the country, the numbers are even greater: 277 in Florida, 260 in Texas, a total of almost 2,000 nationwide. The way has been cleared for the first California execution since Aaron Mitchell's in 1967, now expected to take place in early 1989. It's time for me to spell out just what I learned—as a governor and as a man—from those fifty-nine decisions on Death Row and from my ongoing research into the subject.

Specifically, I reaffirmed what I already knew in 1963: that the death penalty is no deterrent to capital crime, and might even be just the opposite; that it pollutes and clogs up the entire criminal justice system and has a negative impact on the civil legal apparatus.

THE DEATH PENALTY IS NO DETERRENT

The bottom line for some proponents of capital punishment is that, at the very least, the person executed will never kill, rape or kidnap anyone ever again. It's hard to argue with that, especially in view of the Edward Simon Wein case. But figures gathered by many sources, including writers Joe Gunterman and Trevor Thomas, prove how much of an oddity the Wein case really was. "In California, during the period from 1945 through 1982," these two men write in *This Life We Take*, "some 2,527 convicted murderers were back on the streets, paroled from California prisons. During those 37 years, only 27 of those men—or 1.08%—were returned to prison with a new conviction for first degree murder. . . . During those same years, there were about 44,000 murders in California. Clearly, even if all 2,527 paroled murderers had been executed instead, the impact on the number and rate of murders in the state would have been negligible. And the state would itself have killed 2,500 more people not guilty of a new murder in order to get at the 27 who were."

As for the very existence of the death penalty acting as a deterrent against capital crimes, virtually every study ever made proves that it has no such effect. In America, thirteen states have either abolished the death penalty completely or else severely limited it to crimes such as treason or the killing of a police officer or prison guard. But the murder rates in these states have not risen sharply; indeed, they tend to be lower than in states that have retained the death penalty. Many of these abolitionist states, like Kansas, New York, and West Virginia, border on other states that still have the death penalty. If would-be murderers in Pennsylvania or Oklahoma really were frightened by the possibility of execution, all they would have to do was drive a few miles to commit their crimes in the more liberal air of a state that they knew wouldn't kill them. But crime statistics in bordering states with and without the death penalty have been almost exactly identical over the last thirty years. Where they have differed to any significant degree turns out to be a point *against* the death penalty. A 1984 study of six hundred executions over a fifty-seven-year period in New York showed that the rate of homicides actually went up in the first two months after each execution. In California in 1966, when there were no executions, there were 897 willful homicides—or 4.7 per every 100,000 population. In 1967, the year Ronald Reagan let Aaron Mitchell die, that number went up to 1,051 homicides—5.4 per 100,000.

But my two favorite proofs that even the most intimate awareness of the inner workings of capital punishment doesn't act as a deterrent against murder concern convicted criminals in California and Ohio. California's first gas chamber was built at San Quentin in 1937, using labor conscripted from the prison. One of the hardest and best workers was a journeyman plumber serving a term for robbery with violence. This man spent weeks installing the system of pipes and gauges which made the chamber work, and was even present at several successful tests as live pigs were quickly killed. He was subsequently released on parole. Within a year, he shot to death three members of his family, was sentenced to death and wound up seated in the very device he had helped to build.

The Ohio story has a similar piquancy. A convicted robber at the state prison there, assigned to maintenance duty in the room that housed the electric chair, decided that it was a most inefficient instrument of death. Because the condemned prisoner was not bound tightly in the chair, sometimes the electrodes did not make perfect contact with the skin, so the massive charge of electricity hopping between the electrodes and the body would produce burns and an odor that witnesses found distasteful. This convict-inventor designed a set of iron clamps to hold the condemned's legs solidly against the electrodes, and the problem was instantly solved.

The robber got time off his sentence for his ingenious service to the state. Out on the street again, he quickly added first-degree murder to his list of crimes, and he wound up dying in the Ohio electric chair—his legs securely clamped to avoid embarrassment.

When you add to these the hundreds of equally true stories about policemen, prosecutors and prison guards—people whose working lives revolve around the death penalty—committing capital crimes and being executed for them, you begin to realize that whatever else it may be, the death penalty is no deterrent.

THE DEATH PENALTY CLOGS AND POLLUTES THE LEGAL SYSTEM

One very good reason why the death penalty is no deterrent to crime is the long period of time that inevitably passes between the sentencing of a criminal and his actual execution. If you or I as a parent threaten a child with some sort of punishment and the child knows that the punishment, should it ever occur, can be delayed for up to ten years by legal maneuvering, that child is certainly less likely to be daunted by our threat—not to mention the yawning credibility gap that is sure to open around our authority as parents.

Yet the average death-penalty case in California now takes seven years to reach its final resolution. Several of the men on San Quentin's Death Row have been there for ten years; a man in Florida was recently executed thirteen years after his original death sentence. John Crooker has written about what it feels like to be under sentence of death, and his term on Death Row was relatively short. But putting aside the mental anguish involved, not only for the condemned but for his family and the family of his victims, we are left with so long a gap between crime and punishment that every possible deterrent aspect of the execution has long since faded away into the mists of history. Most executions rate a few lines on page 10 of even the largest newspapers, far away in terms of time and temper from the front-page coverage their crimes received.

Death-penalty cases and their built-in delays have another, even more serious effect: they threaten to bring our criminal justice system to a grinding halt. I know many judges, including all three of my former clemency secretaries, and they all tell me that too much of their time—up to 80 percent in some cases—is spent dealing with death-penalty writs and appeals as they laboriously wend their way through the tangled venues of the courts.

These private opinions are more than substantiated by public records. Ever since the voters ousted Chief Justice Rose Bird and two other justices considered to be against the death penalty in 1986, the California Supreme Court under its new chief justice, Malcolm Lucas, has been working seven days a week to ease its backlog of capital cases. When Lucas took over in February 1987, there were 171 death-penalty cases before the court. Working at a frenzied pace, the Lucas court managed to decide on 41 capital cases by the end of July 1988—affirming 29 sentences and reversing 12 others. But during those seventeen months, new death-penalty cases continued to pour in, so that by the end of July 1988 the court had 185 capital cases to decide.

And the most worrying part of that story is all the other cases that are getting little or no attention from the California Supreme Court as a result. "As the justices concentrate on reviewing death verdicts, there is widespread concern in California legal circles that the court is being forced to neglect civil cases and that important decisions thus are being delayed," wrote Philip Hager in the *Los Angeles Times* on July 24, 1988. "Cases that could decide far-reaching questions on the rights of fired non-union workers, the scope of state anti-trust law and the ability of unmarried people to sue for the negligence-caused death of a loved one all remain undecided 15 months after being argued before the court. Other cases that could broaden homeowners' insurance coverage for property damage arising partly from earthslides and set new limits on the political activities of the State Bar also remain pending after being argued late last year. . . .

" 'There's no question that the capital backlog is having an adverse impact—but that's the price you pay for having a death penalty,' said UC Berkeley law professor Preble Stoltz. . . . 'The best argument there is for abolishing the death penalty is the effect it has on the system as a whole.' "

California isn't the only state whose legal resources—time, money and physical plant—are being drained by capital cases: Texas, Florida, Louisiana, Mississippi and Georgia report similar delays on all levels. Since death-penalty cases are most often defended by court-appointed lawyers, who tend to be less experienced and less well paid than their colleagues, this lack of experience plus the necessity to take on a larger workload of cases to pay the bills can't help but add to court delays.

Supporters of capital punishment argue that the process takes as long as it does because of all the built-in protections against killing the innocent. My short reply to that is a familiar barnyard epithet. A study by two law professors published in 1987 in the *Stanford Law Review* showed that 350 innocent men were sentenced to death in the United States in the twentieth century, and that 23 of those were executed before the mistake was discovered. The authors of this study admitted that 350 was a very conservative figure, because they used only cases where the real murderer was found or the state admitted its mistake. In Florida, Joseph Green Brown was freed from prison in 1987, fourteen years after he was sentenced to die for a murder he did not commit. Every governor and attorney general and prosecutor knows of at least one such case. To my knowledge, I never let an innocent person go to his death in California, but as district attorney and attorney general I did supervise the prosecution of at least two cases that later turned out to involve the wrong man. Luckily, these mistakes were discovered in time to acquit or parole the innocent parties, but the cases could easily have gone the other way.

So the long delays common to all death-penalty cases don't necessarily protect the innocent. And they certainly don't guarantee racial equality either. About 53 percent of all the people executed in this country since 1930 have been black. Of those executed for rape, that figure jumps to 89 percent. Despite a very controversial U.S. Supreme Court ruling in April 1987, that the state of Georgia—which kills about twice as many blacks as whites—was not discriminating in specific cases, dozens of reputable studies show that the race of the victim as well as that of the criminal plays a vital part in deciding whether a murderer lives or dies. A 1980 survey by William Bowers and Glenn Pierce concluded that, in Georgia, blacks who killed whites were thirty-three times more likely to receive the death penalty than blacks who killed blacks; in Texas, blacks who killed whites were eighty-four times more likely to get death sentences. Another study by David Baldus found that killers of black victims, whether they were white or black themselves, were punished by death less than one-tenth as often as were killers of white victims. The only possible conclusion to be drawn from all of this is that the death penalty places a higher value on a white life than it does on a black one.

A final damage done to the legal system and the fabric of society by the death penalty is the way it spends public money. Back in the "good old days" of capital punishment, in the 1930s and 1940s when a prisoner could be tried and executed in under a year, at least the argument that it was cheaper to kill him than feed and house him for life could find a few supporters. Now even that has changed. Recent studies show that it can easily cost a state a million dollars or more to carry an indigent prisoner—and most murderers tend to fall into this category—through a jury trial and the years of appeals and delays before his execution. One of the studies that convinced New Yorkers not to return to the death penalty in 1982 had the total cost of trial and appeals pegged at $1.8 million—more than twice what it would cost to keep even the youngest and hungriest prisoner alive and behind bars for the rest of his life.

WHAT CAN BE DONE

Despite the best efforts of anti–capital-punishment groups and individual activists to bring this kind of information to as wide an audience as possible, I'm sure that the death penalty will not be voted out of existence in the forseeable future. Fear and guilt are at work here: legitimate fear of crime and the guilt of daring to take a human life that tends to build up around the death penalty such a protective shield of delays. I'm not convinced that the people of California, or of the other thirty-six states that have a death penalty, will ever be able to put aside those perfectly valid emotions that all of us have when we hear about a particularly vicious murder and vote for abolition. As long as handguns are so easily available, our murder rates will continue to climb, regardless of how many executions take place in California, Texas, Louisiana, Florida and Georgia in 1989 and 1990. I think that the death penalty will remain on the books in those states, and that any changes or improvements will have to come about in spite of it.

This isn't as gloomy a prognosis as it might at first seem. South Dakota has had a death penalty since 1978, but that state's lower courts have managed to avoid the issue by the simple expedient of not once imposing a death sentence. Those courts seem satisfied with giving convicted murderers life sentences without the possibility of parole. So far, there has been no ground swell of indignation from the citizens who voted for capital punishment.

The sentence of life without possibility of parole brings with it some serious problems of its own. As I've already mentioned, certain prosecutors have always been able to frighten jurors into voting for the death penalty by reminding them that such a thing as life without parole doesn't really exist, that somewhere down the road a softheaded governor or a misguided legislature could still return these convicted prisoners to the streets. These worries are certainly not without historic precedent: each of us has some favorite horror story about the killer-rapist turned loose to kill and rape again. What we need is some way to insure that a sentence of life without parole cannot be tampered with except under the most extraordinary of circumstances.

The existence of a life-without-parole sentence can also save court time and taxpayers' money if used as a guarantee in return for a guilty plea. The irony here is that in order for such a guarantee to be effective, the state also has to have a death-penalty law on the books—to motivate a murderer to give up his right to a full trial.

There are other reforms we can hope for short of abolition. As I discussed in Chapter Four, the laws about what constitutes legal sanity still cry out for modification. I continue to believe that if the psychiatrists who examined Edward Simon Wein hadn't been concentrating their focus on the narrow issue of whether or not he was legally sane, they might have discovered in time—as did his fellow prisoners—just how disturbed he really was.

162

In the area of reform, a group called the Crime Victims' California Justice Committee has recently made what I feel are some very valuable suggestions. This group is not anti–capital-punishment, and only a few of its suggested reforms directly relate to the death penalty. But by implementing its reforms—such as eliminating the postindictment preliminary hearing, making lawyers who represent indigent defendants more financially responsible for unconscionable delays, and simplifying the practice of examining jurors—some of the major clogs in the criminal justice system will be cleared away. What will happen then is that nothing will stand in the way of California's first execution in twenty-two years. There will be no more courts to fall back on, no more delays to take comfort from. A governor will once again have to say yes or no; this man must live or die. With more than 230 men awaiting execution, once that machine starts again, it will have to work overtime. Even killing them two at a time, two or three times a week, it would still take a year to get rid of the backlog. Then and only then would people begin to see the death penalty in all its naked ugliness . . .

I am eighty-three years old as I write these words. I've done many things during my life that have given me a great deal of pleasure and pride, and a few things that I'd either like to forget or to have another chance at. But the longer I live, the larger loom those fifty-nine decisions about justice and mercy that I had to make as governor. They didn't make me feel godlike then: far from it; I felt just the opposite. It was an awesome, ultimate power over the lives of others that no person or government should have, or crave. And looking back over their names and files now, despite the horrible crimes and the catalog of human weaknesses they comprise, I realize that each decision took something out of me that nothing—not family or work or hope for the future—has ever been able to replace.

Index

165

INDEX

Warren, Earl, xiii, 24, 25, 31, 59, 104, 105
Wein, Edward Simon, xvi, 30, 31, 84, 90–105, 155, 162
Welsh, James, 60
Welter, Jack, 41
West Germany, abolition of death penalty in, 44
West Virginia, abolition of death penalty in, 156
Whitehorn, Norman, 132–35
Williams, Dr., 60

Winter Olympics (1960), 38, 42
Winterstein, Ralph, 108–9
Wisconsin, abolition of death penalty in, 44
Wolfe, Jim, 26, 27
Woodfield, William Read, 48–50
Woodmansee, Charles, 103
World War II, 55–57, 63–64, 66, 68, 100
Wright, Donald, 154–55
Wright, Robert, 101–2

Young, M. J., 127, 128

About the Authors

Edmund G. (Pat) Brown was governor of California from 1959 through 1966. Since then, he has been in private practice as a partner in the Los Angeles law firm of Ball, Hunt, Hart, Brown and Baerwitz. His previous books include *Reagan and Reality* (1970).

Dick Adler is a coauthor of *Sleeping with Moscow,* a book about the FBI espionage case involving Richard Miller and Svetlana and Nikolai Ogorodnikov. A former magazine editor, he has written more than five hundred articles for magazines including *Life, Playboy, American Heritage, TV Guide, Los Angeles, Ovation, New York Magazine, California,* and the *London Sunday Times Magazine.*